PRINCIPLES
OF
ADMINISTRATION
FOR
A BAPTIST
ASSOCIATION

PRINCIPLES OF ADMINISTRATION FOR A BAPTIST ASSOCIATION

Allen W. Graves

Broadman Press
Nashville, Tennessee

Dewey Decimal Classification: 267
Subject heading: ASSOCIATIONAL WORK

Library of Congress Catalog Card Number: 77-91268
Printed in the United States of America

PREFACE

This book represents the culmination of lifelong interest and involvement in the work of Baptist associations. Some of my earliest denominational meetings were the regular meetings of the associational BYPU of the Williamson County Baptist Association in Illinois. Through associational activities, we shared in the life and work of churches large and small throughout the association. As pastor, Sunday School Board staff member, and seminary professor, I have held continuing responsibilities in Baptist associations. During the past decade my participation in the Gulfshore Conference and training sessions for directors of missions on the seminary campus have brought me firsthand contacts with many capable and dedicated associational directors of missions and others interested in the work of the association.

This volume is prepared with the hope that it may help equip associational leaders for an even more effective ministry.

Appreciation is expressed to Loyd Corder and the staff of the Home Mission Board for their encouragement and assistance. Mrs. Wes Wilkinson has been a faithful helper in typing the manuscript. To these and all that great host of fellow workers in associations throughout the Southern Baptist Convention we express our gratitude.

Contents

1. The Baptist Association 9

2. The Association as Organization 21

3. Associational Administration 53

4. Administrative Functions—Needs, Objectives, and Plans 59

5. Administrative Functions—Organization and Leadership 71

6. Administrative Functions—Directing, Coordinating, Communicating, Financing, and Evaluating 95

7. Director of Missions 113

1.
The Baptist Association

The first expression of denominational organization for interchurch fellowship among Baptists was the association.

1. Defining the Association

What is a Baptist association? E. C. Watson offered this definition: The Baptist association is a self-determining Baptist interchurch community created and sustained by the churches affiliated with her and responsible to them through their messengers, in which the churches foster their fellowship, their unity in faith and practice, and give and receive assistance in achieving their purpose.[1] A subgroup of the Inter-Agency Council offered this definition:

A Baptist association is a voluntary fellowship shared in by Baptist churches and individual members of these churches . . .

a. Enabling them to be and to do some things cooperatively better than is possible if each works alone;

b. With such structure in the form of programs and organizations as is consistent with, and demanded by, the generally accepted Baptist doctrinal position and the needs of the communities which are served by the churches; and

c. Bound together by a common experience with Christ, a common doctrine, and common needs.

A Baptist association is dependent on and responsible to the churches that create and sustain it. It is autonomous in relation to other Baptist bodies. It is the denominational unit closest to the churches and capable of being the most reflective of their conditions and needs. Functionally, it is one of the channels through which Baptist churches can appropriate for their own use the benefits and resources of a larger fellowship while directing their own resources to areas of need within and beyond the geographic scope of the association.

The Inter-Agency Council Coordinating Committee adopted in 1964 this definition: A Baptist association is a self-determining body whose authority is derived from the actions of messengers elected by Baptist churches.

Usually located in a limited geographical area, these churches have voluntarily associated and have organized for Christian fellowship and cooperation in the advancement of Christ's kingdom. An association is dependent on the churches that create and sustain it, and is autonomous in relation to other Baptist bodies.

To define the association in terms of an annual meeting of messengers does not fit comfortably an organization that has continuous existence throughout the year, carrying on many different kinds of activities. If the only activity of an association is to conduct an annual meeting, then the description of the association as a body composed of messengers is quite appropriate.

As the programs and activities of the association expanded from an annual meeting of messengers from congregations to an organization engaged in ongoing programs throughout the year, its existence was institutionalized by providing for structure and leadership to conduct activities throughout the year. These programs and activities called for a more comprehensive definition of the association, indicating more accurately and fully its scope and nature.

Numerous Baptist historians and theologians affirm the concept that associations are not composed of churches but only of messengers of the churches. Yet, in practice most Baptists think and speak of churches "joining" or "withdrawing," and of the association as accepting or withdrawing fellowship from churches.

Lynn May notes in the Inter-Agency Council statements an implication that "an association is composed of messengers in annual session but also of churches in voluntary fellowship organized for cooperative effort in advancing Christ's kingdom. These definitions emphasize the autonomy of the association, its dependence upon and responsibility to the churches which create and sustain it. Churches in an association remain autonomous bodies, but in this voluntary fellowship recognize their dependence upon cooperative effort with other churches to fulfill their mission as a church." [2]

In Baptist polity each association is autonomous; this means, among other things, that each is free to define itself as it chooses. Perhaps the suggestions given above will be helpful to associations seeking to state or revise their own definition of themselves and their constituency.

2. The Legitimacy of the Association

William J. Cumbie, executive secretary of the Mount Vernon Baptist Association in Virginia, raises some pertinent questions regarding the place and purpose of the association: To whom does it belong? Is it an instrument for the churches as they express their mission interest, or is it an instrument for denominational agencies to use to communicate with the churches? Or is it both? [3] Cumbie's opinion is that "the association is clearly amenable to the churches who constitute it and is their instrument for mission in their immediate area."

A few critics of the association have asserted that the association has outlived its usefulness; that there is nothing the association has done that the state convention or some agency of the Southern Baptist Convention cannot now do better. The author's conviction is that such critics are misguided and misinformed, but their criticisms do deserve an answer.

A. *The pragmatic test of legitimacy.* As we have noted, the association was historically the first denominational unit to emerge. The associations did perform several functions initially that were more appropriately performed by state and national organizations when they were established at a later date. There was a period a generation ago in associational history when their chief role in the minds of many denominational leaders was to serve as "delivery teams" for programs planned and promoted by state and national denominational agencies. The author's conviction is that the association has its own legitimate role, not apart from the state and national conventions, and certainly not apart from the churches, but rather in meaningful and fruitful interdependent relationship with all these groups.

The test of legitimacy should be applied continually to all denominational activities. Is the association meeting current needs as well as the needs for which it has been established? Are the affiliated churches satisfied with the ministry the association is performing? Is the association relating satisfactorily to the state and national denominational groups?

Legitimization for the association comes both from the churches and their leaders and from the larger denominational units. To some extent, legitimization comes also from the general public and other organizations serving the same communities served by the association. Associational leaders should never take for granted that everyone accepts the legitimacy or recognizes the importance of the association. One implicit task of the association is to establish the legitimacy of its activities and its methods of operation. Do the results justify the time, effort, and resources being invested in the association?

Not many readers have any serious questions about the continued existence of the churches, although many would urge renewal and change at many points. Not the same kind of loyalty seems to exist regarding the association. Questions concerning its legitimacy result not in urgent demands for its dissolution but rather in indifference, apathy, and lack of involvement and support. There is a theory of entropy regarding organizations in society which holds that systems tend to "run down." Only when an organization receives more input of energy and support from its environment than it expends is it able to continue to function.

We may conclude that the association exists, and should continue to exist, because it has demonstrated pragmatically its ability to meet some real and continuing needs among Baptists. It would be useful, however, to explore some additional bases for the legitimacy of the association.

B. *Biblical implications.* Although there are no direct references to the association in the Bible, there are definite indications of interchurch consultation and cooperative actions on the part of the young Christian churches described in the New Testament.

Acts 11:1–8 describes a conference in Jerusalem after the visit of Peter to the house of Cornelius, where his host and a number of other Gentiles were converted. Critics in Jerusalem objected to the bringing of Gentile converts into the church without circumcision. In a public meeting, Peter rehearsed the entire sequence of events, after which his critics "Held their peace, and glorified God, saying, 'Then hath God also to the Gentiles granted repentance unto life' " (Acts 11:18).

Acts 15:1–35 contains a lengthy description of what is commonly known as the Jerusalem Conference. The Antioch church sent messengers, including Paul, Barnabas, and other brethren, who discussed matters freely and on an equal basis with the members of the church in Jerusalem. Together they reached a consensus on matters of doctrine and mission policy. James summarized their thinking and the gathered group agreed with the conclusions and proposals James had set forth. The whole incident illustrates the concern of the early church members and leaders for spiritual unity. It indicates the way they reached the consensus and their unwillingness to use coercion, choosing rather to persuade and exhort. It demonstrates how representatives of many churches can achieve a basic unity without insisting on uniformity.

Galatians 2:1–10 may refer to the same Jerusalem Conference or possibly to a similar meeting. Paul's report focuses on mission strategy—the assigning of a ministry to the Jews, another to the Gentiles, and the presenting of an approach to meeting the problems of the poor. Other passages in the New Testament tell of the Antioch offering for famine relief, a general offering among the churches for the poor Christians in Jerusalem, and a reporting of missionary activities and results to those involved in sending out missionaries.

We see then in the New Testament how churches maintained basic unity without requiring uniformity; how counsel and assistance were provided to churches. In their cooperative relationships, they exercised mutual responsibility in the context of freedom. They reached a consensus on doctrinal questions; they produced a workable mission strategy, assumed cooperative ministries, and achieved agreement on areas of responsibility. The churches of the New Testament have by their example of consultation, conference, and correspondence, set forth principles and guidelines useful for those engaged in cooperative Christianity today, whether through associations or other denominational organizations.

C. *The association expressing the nature and mission of the church.* The association demonstrates its legitimacy as it expresses in its life and work the nature and mission of the church. The church cannot be the church, in the full sense of being and doing all that Christ intended, without involving itself along with other Christians who share a common faith and purpose. E. C. Watson suggests that "participating in the life of the association is, for the church, a way of expressing her essential unity in Christ with members of other congregations. Because of what the church is, because of the essential unity of all those in the church who share a like experience in and relationship to Christ, expression of this unity through some sort of fellowship and cooperation beyond the local congregation may not be so much an option as a necessity." [4]

Watson says further that "the nature and mission of church and association are inseparably involved with each other. Churches create associations and join in voluntary cooperation with other churches through them because of what the church is. They do so in order to provide for themselves assistance in accomplishing their purposes. The association, in turn, shares in and derives her nature and mission from that of the church." [5]

The Baptist Association

The association exists because of the needs and desires of the churches. No church can fully express and achieve her own nature and mission except in association with other churches, called like them to a common task.

3. Present Functions of the Association

As we have noted, there is a basic, continuing need for the association in Baptist life and work. Southern Baptists are committed to the principle of local church autonomy, but the past century has seen significant growth in the power and influence of state conventions and the Southern Baptist Convention over the life and work of the churches. This development caused a corresponding decline in the role of the associations. This decline has been somewhat counteracted during the past forty years by renewed emphasis on the association as a basic unit in the promotion of programs initiated largely by SBC agencies. Recent decades have seen the employment of directors of missions by approximately three-fourths of the associations and a considerable expansion of associational services and programs. These dedicated and increasingly well-prepared directors and other associational staff members are able to render services to the churches that cannot be given as effectively by those far removed geographically, and otherwise, from the needs of the churches.

Although modern means of travel and communication make it easier for Baptists to participate in state and national meetings and various training programs, the fact remains that only the association has been able to attract more than token representation from the churches, particularly from among the lay members.

At the Gulfshore Conference on Associational Missions in February of 1963, this writer made the following statement regarding the significance of the association:

> We have gathered here this week not for a wake but for a coming out party. We are not here to gather mournfully around the deathbed of an honored and once useful organization that has outlived its usefulness. We are here to launch new and significant programs for a healthy and vigorous body that will

have some of its greatest days yet ahead. The association can and must fill a vital and indispensable role in the ongoing work of the churches. There are functions which can be performed better by the association than by any other agency of denominational life. The association has a valid role, life, and function uniquely its own. Adjustments may be needed, but the association has its own reasons for being, reasons that may call for adaptation and the development of new and improved ways of fulfilling its ministry to the churches.[6]

Developments in the years since that conference support the convictions stated. Churches need the association to provide benefits through cooperative action not easily available to them when acting independently.

As was true in the first century, churches need some instrumentality for maintaining doctrinal clarity and developing mutual understanding in matters of faith and practice; to encourage and facilitate Christian fellowship through sharing information and experiences; to find answers to practical problems and discover ways of working together to minister to human need.

The association offers to the churches an opportunity to express their nature as a Christian fellowship reaching beyond the boundaries of the local congregation. Through the association, many churches can share in work that can be done cooperatively more effectively than independently.

The association may serve as a channel for the resources of the state convention and the Southern Baptist Convention when there is a need for shared assistance to the churches by these larger bodies. Church leadership training projects may involve joint efforts of the association, the state conventions, and the Southern Baptist Convention. A ministry to an ethnic group, to migrants, to other special groups in an area may utilize the association to make available the resources of other denominational agencies in expertise, personnel, and financial support for programs in the area of the association.

As autonomous Baptist groups, any Baptist agency or program is free to respond to direct requests from churches. Practically, it is usually true that Baptist resources can be utilized most effectively when there are cooperative relationships of state and Southern Baptist agencies with leaders of the association who know well the needs of their area.

Baptist agencies outside the association find that the association is an invaluable instrument in interpreting denominational information to the churches, in providing training for church leaders, and in distributing resources to church leaders to help them in their work.

The association can provide accurate information on local church needs to state and Southern Baptist agencies who desire to help the churches in their work.

The objectives and functions of the association will be discussed in greater detail in Chapter Four in the section on "Determining Needs and Objectives."

4. The Relationships of the Association

As we have noted earlier, the basic relationship of the association is to the churches. The churches express their nature and mission, in part, through the association. In one of the early Baptist confessions of faith in 1644, it was asserted that "although we (the seven churches which participated in the confession) be distinct in our meetings, for conveniency; yet are we one in faith, a fellowship, and communion, holding Jesus Christ for our head and lawgiver, under whose rule and government we desire to walk." [7]

Duke McCall made the following comment:

> The local church is autonomous and capable of functioning fully as the church without dependence upon any human configuration beyond itself. It is not required, however, by its nature to remain independent and autonomous. Indeed the emphasis is not upon it as a discreet unit in society but, rather, upon the mind and purpose of God. Therefore, when circumstances permit, and to the degree they permit, each church will be associated in the larger fellowship of Christians. It must witness to the mind of Christ, yet listen with discrimination and concern to the witness of the larger fellowship. It must invite help and seek to give help to the larger fellowship.[8]

Principles of Administration

Mutual concern of the members of each church for the members of other churches is the essence of Baptist associationalism. Baptist churches relate in the association as equal autonomous bodies, each acting in Christian concern and moral responsibility for the other.

We have noted earlier the biblical examples of the expression of concern by New Testament churches for one another. The history of associations in Baptist life demonstrates and manifests this mutual concern.

Associations also are related to other associations and will exercise Christian concern for other associations in the actions which they take. They will recognize the freedom of each church to determine its own associational relationships.

The association also relates to Baptist state conventions. This relationship involves more than simply being a channel of promotion and information for state programs. There should be multidirectional communication so that the association assists state convention leadership at many points in reporting on the needs of the churches in its particular area and adapting available assistance from the state convention to the needs of its affiliated churches. Subsequent chapters will deal with some specific details of organizational and financial relationships between the association and the state convention.

Most Baptists are familiar with the basic principle of Baptist polity that, unlike some other denominations, the associations, the state conventions, and the Southern Baptist Convention all look back to the local churches for messengers to compose their organizational structures. The state convention is composed of messengers from churches, not messengers from associations. The Southern Baptist Convention is composed of messengers from churches, not of messengers from state conventions or associations. The relationships between associations, state conventions, and the Southern Baptist Convention are those of self-determining bodies, all concerned with assistance to the churches in expressing their basic nature and mission.

The association also has relationships to its community and to the business, political, social and welfare agencies in the community. It may also have relationships with other religious groups of either regional or national scope.

Relationships with these various groups grow out of a concern for and pursuit of common goals and objectives. Cooperation has been a basic characteristic of Baptists throughout most of their history. This factor has sometimes been obscured by those periods of insecurity and suspicion which has led some Baptist groups to behavior which has the critical description of "narrow-minded Baptists." Cooperation in achieving Christian objectives is appropriate and desirable where it does not involve compromise of Christian convictions and biblical truths.

In recent decades, governmental, and volunteer agencies outside the church have assumed responsibility for many of the services to people formerly carried on by churches. Associations can assist churches in discovering such resources for ministry to people in need and seek to channel the resources of the association and related churches into meeting unmet needs of people rather than duplicating available services from other sources.

An illustration of this kind of relationship may be seen in the work of the Gaston Baptist Association in North Carolina. The director of missions led in the developing of a manual of community services provided by all kinds of agencies in the area of the association. The booklet proved to be such a useful item that the local chamber of commerce has assumed responsibility for duplicating copies and distributing them in the community. When human needs are discovered by welfare personnel and no government resources are available, the Baptist associational office is contacted to help in meeting the human needs.

NOTES

1. E. C. Watson, *Associational Base Design* (Atlanta: Home Mission Board, 1972), p. 33.

2. Lynn E. May Jr., *The Work of the Baptist Association, An Integrative Study* (Atlanta: Home Mission Board, 1969), p. 23.

3. William J. Cumbie, "Baptist Polity: A Survey of Issues and Trends from the Associational Perspective," *Search*, I, 2, Winter, 1971, p. 20.

4. E. C. Watson, p. 14.

5. *Ibid.*, p. 13.

6. *Report of Conference on Associational Missions*, February 11–15, 1963, Gulfshore Baptist Assembly (Atlanta: Home Mission Board, 1963), pp. 165–166.

7. W. J. McGlothlin, *Baptist Confessions of Faith* (Valley Forge: American Baptist Publications Society, 1911), p. 186f.

8. Duke K. McCall, "Is Absolute Autonomy Desirable," *Search*, I, 2, Winter, 1971, p. 14.

2.

The Association as Organization

Organizations are characteristic of modern society. The association is only one of many organizations which constitute contemporary life. Life in modern America is dominated by large and complex organizations. Most Americans are now born in a hospital, educated in a school, belong to some church, are affiliated with numerous civic, social, and political organizations, and earn their livelihood in some kind of organization. Southern Baptists have been in step with this pattern of American life in their ability to organize millions of people to accomplish large-scale tasks.

Multiplication of large organizations and our growing involvement in many of them has brought about one of the problems of our age: that of reconciling the autonomy of the individual and our concept of political democracy with the often overwhelming impact of large organizations in society. Up until about a century ago, Baptists were very wary and suspicious of large ecclesiastical organizations. They were fearful that their freedom and autonomy, both as individuals and as local churches, might be endangered by organizational involvement.

One aspect of any organization is the centralization of power in the hands of those selected to lead. Baptist denominational polity has provided wisely for a system of checks and balances for democratic accountability and control.

Among the painful lessons of history has been the discovery that bestowing of power to facilitate the accomplishment of organizational objectives may open the door to the misuse of power by those to whom it is given. Power can be exercised to silence the prophetic voice, to thwart proposals for needed change and to perpetuate the status quo.

Denominational organizations can also suffer from rigidity and inflexibility. We can become preoccupied with organizational mechanics and procedures and overlook the basic objectives for which the organization was originally established. Elaine Dickson has warned of the dangers of institutionalism.

> Institutionalism is an unbalanced emphasis on organization and operation. Institutionalism is overconcern with means rather than ends. Institutionalism results in loss of flexibility, the tendency to cling to old patterns, and stubborn refusal to change.
>
> Is eleven o'clock on Sunday morning the best time for congregational worship? Maybe so. Maybe not. The most important thing is worship, not when or how it is conducted.
>
> Is a two-week revival the best method for giving emphasis to witness in the life of a church? Sometimes yes. Sometimes no. A revival as a method is not sacred. Bringing men to God through Jesus Christ is . . . .
>
> Churches will continue to be institutions, but they do not have to give way to institutionalism.[1]

Dickson asserts further that "the most challenging job for Southern Baptists in the 70's is to become open, to let the spirit of God invade their schedules, methods, and plans, and to let God remold them from within. . . . Persons critical of present organizations and methods should produce new ones that focus on helping accomplish God's mission in the world."[2]

To maintain denominational organizations that are both efficient and democratic requires careful selection and continuing democratic control of the central bureaucracy of both paid staff members and elected volunteer leaders who direct the affairs of denominational agencies and organizations.

Historically as organizations have increased in size, geographic

The Association as Organization

spread, and heterogenity of membership, the tendency has frequently been to decline both in efficiency and effectiveness. Some of the alienation expressed in recent decades by the younger generation toward the "establishment," whether political, economic, or religious, has been a reaction to what they have felt to be the unresponsiveness of personnel in large organizations to the needs of individuals. A prevailing problem in many associations is the apathy, if not outright antagonism, toward any kind of denominational structure. It is important, therefore, if one is to serve effectively as an associational leader, to understand both the cause and ways of preventing such attitudes from developing. Further suggestions will be found later in this book.

Even though organizations seem to be assuming major roles in contemporary society, organizations have been a feature of religious life throughout human history. The story of the Exodus is the exciting record of the transformation of a motley throng of slaves into an organized "people of God" prepared to function in specific ways. Jethro proved to be of great help to Moses by bringing about better organization and administration. He serves as the prototype of all organizational consultants (Ex. 18:17–27).

The New Testament records many manifestations of organized activity. The church began with an organized band of twelve gathered about Jesus. Groups of seventy were organized and sent out two by two by Jesus on a witnessing campaign, and they brought back reports to him. After Christ's ascension, one hundred and twenty believers gathered in the upper room for worship, prayer, ministry, and organized activity. The group rapidly expanded, yet maintained some recognizable boundaries. The book of Acts speaks of people being added daily to the church. Organizational structure in the early church tended to be quite flexible as we note the selection of a successor to Judas, in the selection of the seven (Acts 6:1–6), the scattering of the Christians and formation of new congregations, the gathering of representatives from the scattered congregations to deal with emerging problems (Acts 15:1–35), and the emergence of planned missionary outreach, et cetera. The forms and functioning of emerging organizations in Christian history were determined by a combination of imitation, improvisation, and innovation.

Churches today, like most other segments of society, have developed more numerous and complex organizational structures. Southern Baptists have been characterized by intensive organizational activity.

Over the last two decades the Southern Baptist Convention, and most of its agencies, has conducted intensive and comprehensive studies of its organizations with a view for clarifying objectives, assigning program responsibilities, and improving both efficiency and effectiveness. The Committee to Study the Total Southern Baptist Program, authorized by the Southern Baptist Convention in 1956, used the services of a management consultant firm and over a period of several years brought numerous recommendations regarding the organization and functioning of the Convention.

Southern Baptist Convention agencies and state Baptist conventions engaged in similar studies. Never before in Baptist history had Baptist organizations been so extensively examined, inspected, evaluated, and contemplated. This was done primarily to achieve greater efficiency, better coordination, and more results.

Some associations have engaged in serious self-study, evaluation and long-range planning.[3] The suggestions in this volume may be found useful in making such an examination of an association and developing recommendations for improved organizational functioning.

1. Understanding Organizations

Organizations are useful. They do things for us. As needs have developed, we have established organizations to meet these needs. Through organizations people establish relationships by which they can work together more effectively. As noted earlier, most of us spend increasing amounts of time in organizations of various kinds; in hospitals, schools, churches, businesses, social and political organizations, civic clubs, transportation systems, et cetera. It is as important for people today to learn organization theory and practice as it was important for

The Association as Organization

their forefathers to learn farming, for organizations are society's chief instruments for achieving its purposes in our modern world.[4]

Organizing is a process and it involves establishing structure or forms for ordered relationships. Relationships are more important than structure. Scholars from many fields can aid us in understanding our relationships with church and denominational organizations, whether our concern is in establishing new organizations or improving those now in existence. Psychologists help us to understand individual behavior. Social psychologists can aid us in understanding the behavior of small groups. The sociologists can throw light on large groups and the interactions among groups within the social structure.[5] Through training in human relations skills, associational leaders can become more sensitive to human needs and feelings, and can come to recognize the importance of delegating responsibility and securing participation on the part of all organization members. A well-balanced associational organization is like a complete human body with all its correlated functions: heartbeat, circulation, respiration, renewal, growth, and activity.

We may make a larger contribution to the achievement of associational goals by more careful structuring of the associational organization in utilizing and rewarding the skills, talents, and interests of the members of the affiliated churches. Careful structuring helps individuals in performing those tasks which the churches look to the association to achieve. When the association is engaged in matters important to the churches and their individual members, they will have a much greater enthusiasm for helping achieve associational objectives.

No matter what one has to do with an organization—whether one is going to study it, work in it, administer it, criticize it, subvert it, or use it in the interest of another organization—it is helpful to have a clear understanding of the nature of organizations and how they function. This chapter seeks to provide some helpful perspectives on the association as an organization. Such insight may be useful in dealing with the numerous organizations one encounters in contemporary life as well as bringing about a better understanding of the association itself.

Principles of Administration

2. The Value of Organization Theory

Some readers may have less interest in organization theory than in more practical "how-to-do-it" techniques of associational work. Yet, sometimes nothing is so practical and helpful as a good theory. One of the tests of good theory is its practical implications. An understanding of organization theory can help associational leaders find and utilize the best techniques, organizational structures, and procedures for accomplishing the work of the association.

The association does not deal exclusively with individuals, but much more frequently with other organizations such as churches, state conventions, SBC agencies, county planning boards, public schools, and other community and denominational organizations. Understanding organization theory helps a person to analyze the association and the many other organizations with which one may be related.

Knowing how an organization functions, being able to analyze its problems and its needs will enable associational leaders to choose the specific techniques and the appropriate programs needed to achieve associational goals. If it is known how voluntary religious organizations normally function, one will be able to anticipate the steps that will need to be taken, and the organizational structures that will need to be established to accomplish specific associational tasks.

A little learning can be a dangerous thing. Anyone reading literature on administration will have encountered the conventional wisdom that most organizational problems are "people problems" and that good leadership is the answer. It should be noted, however, that many "people problems" and "leadership problems" are due really to poor organizational structure. There may be something about the way the associational organization is structured and the way it is trying to function that causes people and leaders to have problems. People's attitudes are often shaped as much by the organization in which they work as by their preexisting attitudes and experiences.

The Association as Organization

3. What Is an Organization?

An organization is a group of people banded together to work toward a common goal. When people with common purposes join together, the result is that there is usually an organization to get things done. Organization is a way of dividing responsibility for the work to be done and coordinating the activities of many different persons in achieving desired goals. An organization is a system of relationships and consciously coordinated activities among specific individuals concerned with the attainment of specific goals. When goals are diffused, it is difficult to get a group organized. As the organization develops, various members assume or are assigned particular roles or responsibilities in some form of division of labor or specialization among the organization members. The group interacts with each other and with their environment in established behavior patterns.

As soon as it is established, an organization has two aims: the accomplishment of the original purpose for which it was formed, and the maintenance and management of the organization so that it can survive and function as a viable entity.

Donald Metz reports in his book, *New Congregations*, that most of the six new congregations he studied gave priority to survival goals rather than to mission goals. Church members felt that the survival goals clearly and obviously were necessary and they felt that the denominational executives were also more concerned with the successful achievement of survival goals by the new congregations. Metz found that "the early emphasis on survival goals, however, has consequences that make it difficult to alter the congregation's orientation at a later stage . . . the commitments, both financial and in participation, to the buildings, equipment, and program soon force the more active members to direct their energies to maintenance functions." [6]

Metz concluded that "the possibility of orienting an organization around formal (mission) goals is enhanced where the professional leadership is sufficiently secure that they need not establish an image of success by promoting survival goals." [7]

An association exists for services it can render to its affiliated churches, to the community and to other denominational units. Maintenance of associational organization is useful only as it contributes to these services, rendered both internally and externally.

A church or an association is related to several different categories of persons. An association, for example, is related to the messengers of the churches affiliated with it. It is related also to the persons they seek to serve in the churches, in the larger community where they render mission ministries and other services, and in other denominational agencies such as state and SBC groups. The association exists for the mutual benefit of the churches and the church members. It also exists to minister to persons outside that membership as it seeks to evangelize, minister, instruct, and influence public opinion, et cetera.

4. Three Perspectives on Organization Theory

For the past seventy-five years, various organizational theorists have attempted to develop concepts or models to help understand better the structure and function of organizations. Three basic concepts or perspectives have emerged, each of the later concepts building on or reacting to the previous concept. The three ways of looking at organizations are not mutually exclusive. Frequent similarities and overlappings in the theories and also some partial conflicts among the points of view are offered by the three groups. More work needs to be done to develop a single, comprehensive theory of organizations, particularly an adequate organization theory applicable to church and denominational organizations. This brief look at some of the prevailing theories may be helpful in gaining some insight into the way we now think organizations are likely to function. To benefit by the point of view provided by each of the three major groups of organizational theorists, they are described briefly below. These groups may be designated as: A. The Rational System Approach, also known as Scientific Management; B. The Natural System

The Association as Organization

Approach, sometimes called the Human Relations Approach; C. The Open System Approach, sometimes called the Behavioral Science Approach.

These three groups and the designations proposed represent an oversimplification of the extensive research and current writing in the fields of organizational theory and the various behavioral sciences giving attention to the problems of human organizations. The churches and denominations have been affected in various ways as these concepts of organizations have emerged, as we note below.

A. *The rational system.* Under this heading we are including the scientific management theories of F. W. Taylor, Henri Fayol, and others; along with the concepts of bureaucracy stated by Max Weber. Around the beginning of the twentieth century, interest began to develop, particularly in business and industry, on the technical and productional level of organizations. Men like F. W. Taylor were seeking to find "the one best way" to perform any task efficiently and economically. They then sought to teach each one in the organization to perform his given tasks according to rigidly prescribed procedures. Persons in the organizations, participants or employees, were viewed essentially as machines to be programmed and controlled. Maximum performance was assumed to be enhanced by restricting all outside influences on individuals involved. Great emphasis was placed on the setting of specific goals and establishing clearly defined rules and procedures for achieving those predetermined goals. Theoretically, organizations could be rationally constructed to achieve any given goal. This point of view is still widely held today, despite the additional insights that have emerged from other schools of thought.

In the scientific management or rational system, members of an organization are assigned or assume differentiated roles or specializations. The goal of these theorists was to make more efficient machines out of the people involved. The roles or "job descriptions" became quite rigidly described and rules of procedure emerged to guide the production and decision-making processes. An organization of this kind is known as a bureaucracy. Max Weber has described how such bureaucracies operate.[8] Operations research is the contemporary form of the scientific management point of view.

Most denominational organizations are structured on the bureaucratic model described by Weber. Many denominational executives, like leaders in business and industry, are thoroughly committed to the central concept of bureaucracy—efficiency. Weber's bureaucratic model sees efficiency being assured by (1) the structure and function of the organization, (2) the means of rewarding effort, and (3) the provisions for the protection of individuals.

Too many church and denominational leaders have assumed that "what is good for General Motors is also good for the church" without examining the underlying theological, psychological and sociological presuppositions of bureaucracy.

Warren G. Bennis describes bureaucracy as "a useful social invention that was perfected during the industrial resolution to organize and direct the activities of a business firm . . . Its anatomy consists of the following components:

- a well-defined chain of command
- a system of procedures and rules for dealing with all contingencies relating to work activities
- a division of labor based on specialization
- promotion and selection based on technical competence
- impersonality in human relations

It is the pyramid arrangement we see on most organizational charts." [9] Bennis predicts "the coming death of bureaucracy," saying that "just as bureaucracy emerged as a creative response to a radically new age (the industrial revolution), so today new organizational shapes are surfacing before our eyes." [10] Bennis sees "four relevant threats to bureaucracy in (1) rapid and unexpected change, (2) growth and size, (3) increasing diversity, and (4) change in managerial behavior, involving:

- a new concept of *man* based on increased knowledge of his complex and shifting needs which replaces an over-

The Association as Organization

simplified, innocent, push-button idea of man.

- a new concept of *power* based on collaboration and reason, which replaces a model of power based on coercion and threat.
- a new concept of *organizational values* based on humanistic-democratic ideals, which replaces the depersonalized, mechanistic value system of bureaucracy." [11]

However, other scholars, perhaps more realistic, assert that bureaucracy is likely to be the prevailing organizational pattern for some time to come. These latter scholars lament the fact that bureaucracy has become a "dirty word," both to the average person and to many specialists on organization. With many the term *bureaucracy* has become associated with the idea of red tape and involves unnecessary complications in getting things done. It suggests rigid rules and regulations, a hierarchy of offices, narrow specialization of personnel, an abundance of offices or units which can hamstring those who want to get things done, impersonality, resistance to change. Yet, every organization of any significant size is bureaucratized to some degree.[12]

Perrow noted three bases for bureaucratization: (1) the need for specialization within the organization—the assigning of particular responsibilities to specific individuals, (2) the need for control over the extra-organizational influences upon members of the organization, and (3) the need to stablize the effects of a changing environment.[13]

Perrow acknowledged, however, that "bureaucratization is valuable only up to a certain point; that there are some occasions when the efficiency it produces is not worth the inflexibility with which it is associated." [14]

Morton F. Rose, staff member at the Sunday School Board in an evaluation of how Christian leadership functions in a bureaucracy, commented that "the basic philosophy of organization which gives the best setting for accomplishing the Christian and synergistic objectives is one which assists leadership to serve as life-giving and growth agents for individuals as they work together to achieve organizational goals. This would accomplish the purpose that brought them together in the organization. The bureaucratic organization is the poorest type of organization to do this." [15]

Peter F. Rudge discussed bureaucratic theory (which he labels "classical") in theological terms, being one of the few authors to deal with the issue of inconsistency of bureaucracy with Christian theology. Rudge concluded, that "the classical (bureaucratic) theory is generally inimical to the Christian faith." [16] In addition to bureaucratic (classical) organization, Rudge identified four other organizational patterns: (1) *traditional* organization, in which leadership functions as the elder, wise and sacred voice of tradition which is the source of wisdom, the nurturer and guardian of tradition; (2) *charismatic* organization, in which leadership functions as the superior, enlightened prophets who have unique and special inspiration; (3) *human relations* organization, in which leadership functions as a group of leaders who seek to make everyone happy (leaders are sensitive, permissive, nondirective, and seek always to create the right atmosphere); and (4) *systemic* organizations, in which leadership functions as expert technicians who interpret the environment, clarify goals, and monitor change.

Rational (scientific management or bureaucratic) theorists, such as Henri Fayol in France, began not with the worker but with the manager, seeking to devise a set of principles and guidelines for the administrator who supervised the ongoing work of the organization. These theorists focused on such matters as coordination, the "scalar" principle linking subordinates to a supervisor in the typical pryamid of an organizational chart. They were concerned with the "span of control" which sought to determine how many people could be supervised efficiently by a single individual, the concept of unity of command, hierarchy of authority and a procedure for handling exceptions. They were concerned about finding appropriate methods for grouping tasks in departments, with the line-staff differentiation, and other methods of specialization.

Associational leaders can profit by a study of rational organization theory. Rational theorists stress the importance of goals, a significant

The Association as Organization

emphasis for associational leaders. The more specific the definition of goals, the easier it is to design an organizational structure and procedure to achieve the goals. When goals are uncertain, diffused, or not clearly stated, much time will be spent in the association seeking consensus on what the association and its various subgroups are supposed to do and how to get organized to do it.

Goals contribute to, but don't guarantee achievement. Goals help to keep the organization headed in the right direction. If one does not know where he wants to go, any road will do. Goals rule out unproductive alternatives.

There is a danger that an organization may become absorbed in goal setting to the neglect of goal reaching. Planning is a prelude to, not a substitute for work, as will be noted in Chapter Four.

While the scientific management point of view proved very useful, it soon became apparent that it had some weaknesses and omissions. It failed to take adequately into account the interpersonal and intergroup relationships each participant brought with him into any organization. It failed to deal with the larger social structures, the ecological context, the total environment, and their impact on organizational functioning. Attention was focused too exclusively on what happens within a given organization. It seemed to assume that if you devised a good plan, set up a good organization chart, job descriptions, et cetera, that the organization would automatically function effectively. The truth is that it takes more than a good plan for an organization to work well. No organization has complete control of its members. They bring themselves as whole persons to any organizational task and these external relationships must not be ignored in the organizational plans and structures. In effect, the rational viewpoint is irrational because it ignores the emotional or nonrational behavior of organizational participants.

To ignore nonlogical behavior is to overlook an important aspect of any group functioning.

Much criticism of the rational-bureaucratic-scientific management theory of organization and administration is directed at the basic assumptions of this view which Douglas McGregor summarized in his famous "Theory X," which assumes that: The average human being has an inherent dislike for work and will avoid it if he can. Most people must be coerced, controlled, directed, and threatened with punishment to get them to put forth adequate effort toward the achievement of organizational objectives. The average human being prefers to be directed, wishes to avoid responsibility, has relatively little ambition, and wants security above all.[17]

McGregor concluded that "so long as the assumptions of Theory X continue to influence managerial strategy, we will fail to discover, let alone utilize the potentialities of the average human being." [18]

B. *The human relations point of view.* Reacting to the inadequacies of the rational or scientific management point of view, organization theorists moved to a "natural system" or human relations point of view. Michels, Mayo, Selznick, Parsons, and Simon are among the leaders in this group of theorists. They noted that organizations are made up of both rational and nonrational elements. They pointed out that most organizations, rather than having clearly defined and specified goals, actually had very diffuse and multiple goals. Cyert and March pointed out that organizational goals are not only multiple but may also be conflicting and can be pursued all at once or in sequence.[19] Goals are hard to observe and measure, and it is difficult to distinguish between individual goals and organization goals.

The natural system theorists saw organizations emerging naturally from the associations of people who have common needs, interests, or objectives. They focus on people in the work group, on the behavior of people in organizations. In the Hawthorne studies and subsequent research, Mayo and his colleagues discovered the following: 1. The amount of work carried out by a worker (and hence the organizational level of efficiency and rationality) is not determined by his physical capacity but by his social "capacity." 2. Noneconomic rewards play a central role in determining the motivation and happiness of the worker. 3. The highest specialization is by no means the most efficient form of division of labor.

The Association as Organization

4. Workers do not react to management and its norms and rewards as individuals but as members of groups.[20]

The natural system theorists concluded that all formal organizations seem to share one overriding goal, that of survival as a system. "Organizations exist to persist." They cite examples of organizations beginning to experience difficulty or encountering changed circumstances actually changing their original goal in order to survive as a functioning organization. One illustration might be the March of Dimes, created to fight polio. When medical discoveries led to the conquering of that disease as a major threat, the organization shifted its focus to birth defects. This was of course, a perfectly legitimate and socially useful action. It does illustrate, however, the characteristic of all organizations to survive if possible. Leaders who have worked in an organization for many years, doing things in a routine way, are less willing to develop new organizational patterns and new approaches to the basic task of the organization, particularly if it threatens their positions of leadership. Illustrations of this principle may be found in many associations.

The natural system or human relations theorists placed more emphasis on the behavior of the individual in the group. Within organizations they noted that members participate as whole persons, not just performing their prescribed roles. Each member brings new problems and challenges to the organization because of the needs of his own personality, and his established habits and commitments to groups outside the organization. Because of their own personal goals and attitudes, organization members may resist the demands made upon them by the organization. Therefore, the winning of consent is a basic function of organization leadership. Organizations are cooperative systems constituted of individuals interacting as whole persons in relation to the formal system of coordination provided by the organization. Just as the individual members function as whole persons, so the organization (i.e., the Baptist association) functions as a totality, reacting to the influences upon it from its environment, such as expectations from the churches, the state convention, SBC agencies, or forces in its community.

Principles of Administration

The human relations theorists noted how often actual behavior of people in organizations seemed to hinder or thwart the carefully made plans of leaders, often because of commitments of individual members to other groups in the community. They tried to find out what kept an organization from functioning effectively and came to see the importance of the interdependence of the component parts. Any changes introduced have ramifying consequences for the whole organizational system. The natural system theorists regard the organization as an organically growing whole which cannot easily be modified. Surgeons may be able to make minor changes in the human body, such as straightening a nose or lengthening a leg bone, but major modifications such as organ transplants are difficult and perilous. So it is with changing human organizations.

Planners and change agents must take into account this characteristic behavior of organizations. The ill-fated attempt a few years ago to introduce a new name and new philosophy for the Church Training program among Southern Baptists illustrates this point.

The natural system theory focuses attention on the importance of spontaneous, unplanned, informal patterns of belief and behavior that arise within the organizations, however carefully and rationally their activities have been planned.

In summary, associational leaders can profit from the insights provided in the "human relations" approach through greater awareness of what motivates commitment and high performance levels in associational work. However, this need not cause us to reject all of the principles and theories of the earlier rational theorists using the scientific administration approach. We need, for example, to state clearly supervisory and reporting relationships of both paid staff members and volunteer leaders. We need to limit the span of control to the normal range of the ability of any one leader to supervise a given number of people reporting directly to him. The number of people one is able to supervise directly will depend upon the kind of task being carried out. Job descriptions and policy manuals, if democratically developed and properly

The Association as Organization

used, can enhance associational effectiveness.

C. *The open system perspective.* The natural system of organizational analysis may well have overreacted to the weaknesses of the rational or scientific management view. Both views have useful insights. The search continues for a more adequate theory or system, not only to enable us to better understand organizations but also to help us utilize them more effectively. Consider the following theory:

The most recent development in organizational theory is called the open system approach. Some scholars relate this development to the "behavioral science era" in organization theory. One leader in this emerging movement, von Bertalanffy, became concerned over the compartmentalization of knowledge and the lack of free communication between organization theorists working in the different branches of science. He sought to establish some linkages to get those dealing with similar problems to break out of their cocoons and build bridges for communication and interchange. He suggested that the behavior of organizations or entities is a function of their "systemness," and is related to the degree, type, and nature of their organization. The open system theorists distinguish between open and closed systems, meaning that open systems are continually involved in interchange with their environments.[21] They would help us to see that we cannot understand the Baptist association by looking only at its internal structure and function, but must take into account the larger systems in which it functions. The behavior of forces in these other supersystems or subsystems continually affect, restrict, and determine the actions of the association.

An important concept of the open system is "entropy," which refers to the tendency of organizations to move toward disorganization to "run down" unless continuing effort is exerted to maintain them. Open systems are able to import energy from their environments and thus counteract or postpone entropy. Most associational leaders are well aware of the continuing effort required to keep the associational organizations working effectively.

37

Principles of Administration

Open systems use feedback mechanisms to evaluate their own functioning, enabling the organization to make corrections so as to keep moving toward chosen goals. The information feedback system enables organizational administrators to evaluate continuously the relationship of actual organizational output or performance with organizational purpose and objectives.

An "open" organizational system exhibits dynamic flexibility and responsiveness to change. Associations, like other denominational organizations, cannot remain static in the midst of changing circumstances and needs. Associational structure should be related to the context in which the association exists and functions. The association's objectives help determine its optimal organization. Structure follows strategy.

In analyzing a Baptist association, an open system theorist would be concerned with the input of the association, the energies, resources, and investments of time, effort, and money. How are these resources utilized in training people, ministering to people, coordinating and communicating, and performing other desired services for the churches? What impact is the work of the association having? What results is it achieving? He would ask, does it require all of the input of resources just to keep the associational organization functioning, just to survive, or are resources being utilized by the organization so that the designed purposes of the association are being achieved?

The open system theorist analyzes the way the association is influenced by its environment and evaluates the impact of new leaders and new members on the structure and values of the association, and the impact of changes in the way state convention and SBC leaders recommend and promote church programs so that organization leaders may discover what actions are not most productive.

The open system theorist recognizes that a given outcome may be the result of any one of a number of different causes. He notes that from a given point of departure may be many different possible outcomes. He also insists that the best way to understand an organization is not by analyzing it piece by piece, but rather to take the whole system into

38

consideration whenever any component elements or relationships are analyzed. As John Donne insisted that "no man is an island," this theorist would say no organization is an island, but is a "part of the main" bound together with constant interacting relationships.

The open system theorist would suggest that we be more concerned with these ongoing relationships than with the official structure of an organization. An organization chart can mislead one if he ignores the constant flow of information, energy, and resources that is constantly being interchanged within any organization and between the organization and its community. The open system theorist sees this continuing relationship with the environment as a source of strength and vitality, not as a threat as many of the rational and natural system theorists view an organization's environment. Through its system of feedback and self-regulation, the association functioning as an open system is able to determine how much energy and resources are needed from its constituency to do its job, to maintain the organization, and to conduct the ministry and services the association is expected to perform in its community. A good associational organization is one that functions productively, that through a sequence of events accomplishes in the lives of participants the objectives, purposes, and goals that the association was established to achieve.

5. Differences in Associations

Associations differ from one another for good and legitimate reasons just as churches and individuals differ. What works well in one association will not necessarily work in all other associations. Where the churches are very much alike—in size, location, staff, programs, et cetera—a more standardized associational program may be possible. But where the churches within the association differ in these respects—when some have paid staffs for educational, music, and youth leadership and others do not; when some are rural and some are urban; when some are small and some are large—the association will need to "custom make" its programs to fit the varying needs of participating churches and members. This requires more time, effort, and resources, but attempting to use the same pattern for all churches will not work successfully.

Each association is different from other associations, from state conventions and from the Southern Baptist Convention. Dogmatic statements, purportedly true of all associations, are likely to be either exceedingly general or quite trivial. Associations undergo continuing change themselves so that the association this year is different from that same association last year. Heraclitus expressed it many centuries ago: "Into this same river you cannot step twice, for other waters are flowing." It is appropriate that associations differ in order to minister effectively to the unique needs of the community each seeks to serve, utilizing the unique combination of resources available there.

Expectations regarding what an association is supposed to do vary widely both within and among those outside the association. If an association is to respond to these varying expectations, its activities cannot be routinized, precisely specified, and rigidly controlled. It must be an open system. More freedom and discretion will be needed by association leaders to respond to emerging requests and needs. The director of missions and other association administrators should make the fullest possible use of capacities of present or potential participants in the association who are members of the affiliated churches. Many projects, task forces, and ad hoc programs can be undertaken by shaping such programs around the special abilities and interests of available personnel in the association.

If there are within the association one or more well qualified Christian social workers, a diagnostic counseling and referral system may be organized to help pastors, parents, and others discover sources of help for people facing social and family problems.

Personnel specialists in community industries may be enlisted by associational leaders in providing vocational guidance. College students may be enlisted to tutor underprivileged children needing academic assistance from caring people.

Some individuals have difficulty adjusting to a more flexible, task force structuring of a church or association. Some are used to having everything highly structured along familiar patterns, with steps clearly specified. When the Southern Baptist Convention served a rather homogeneous population in the South, it was feasible to propose and promote "one best way" of enlarging a Sunday School, raising the budget, or conducting evangelism. Now that the constituency is much more heterogeneous, we must discover many ways to do whatever needs to be done, and recognize that the needs of one community in the inner city may be quite different from those of one in the country. To paraphrase a Vacation Bible School motto from a past generation, "We must learn to do the best we can with what we have where we are for Jesus' sake today."

The pattern of services performed by associations has changed significantly in recent years. Once the chief methodology was planning and conducting large group meetings, one for each church program organization at specified intervals with programs focusing on conferences for leadership development and inspirational messages. Greater emphasis is placed currently on one-to-one consultation of associational leaders with church and denominational leaders, helping to devise particular programs to meet specific local needs in a given congregation or community. Associational leaders are continually finding out about new ways of serving the constituency, and discovering new expectations or opportunities emerging from the constituency. Task forces are recruited often on an ad hoc, temporary basis to function until the particular need is met, after which the particular task force work group may be dissolved and others brought into being, utilizing other participants in many cases, to deal with emerging needs now given priority.

Bennis and Slater entitled their book attempting to describe the organizational patterns of society in the future, *The Temporary Society*.

> The key word for describing their structures is "temporary." There will be adaptive, rapidly changing *temporary systems*. These will be task forces composed of groups of relative strangers with diverse professional backgrounds and skills organized around problems to be solved. The groups will

be arranged on an organic rather than mechanical model, meaning that they will evolve in response to a problem rather than to preset, programmed expectations. People will be evaluated not vertically according to rank and status but flexibly according to competence. Organizational charts will consist of project groups rather than stratified functional groups. Most of these trends have been surfacing for some years in the aerospace, construction, drug, and consulting industries as well as in professional and research and development organizations.[22]

Could this be a description of the Baptist association of the future?

When the environment of any organization is stable and the expectations regarding it are clearly defined and understood, it is possible to follow prescribed procedures, schedules, organizational patterns, et cetera. However, when an association is functioning in a dynamic community with many changes occurring in the community and in the churches, the association needs more flexible, adaptable organization and administrators, able to respond quickly to emerging needs. Creativity and ingenuity are valued more highly than diligent adherence to prescribed routines.

This does not mean that there is complete freedom for everyone to "do his own thing" since there must be some degree of specialization or acceptance of responsibility for particular areas. The new approach seeks to enlist administrators, leaders, committee members, et cetera, who are committed to the goals of the association and seek to respond to needs in their area of responsibility in the most helpful way, utilizing as effectively as possible the available resources whether from within or outside the association.

We tend to think of associations like churches, as enduring organizations with fairly precise boundaries and characteristics which distinguish them from all that is outside. Some churches and denominational groups spend exorbitant amounts of time and energy trying to decide their basis for membership and participation. With the decline of rigid church discipline, churches and denominational organizations are less and less able to control the total lives of those who participate. People come from

The Association as Organization

an environment outside the control of the church or denomination. People tramp in and out with mud on their shoes that they bring in from the outside world. We cannot do a perfect job of selecting the kinds of people that we do admit into the organization and we do not retain them long enough to remake them completely.[23]

The association deals with people. Its processes and activities are designed to change people, to minister to their needs, to equip them for more effective leadership, to enable them more effectively to cope with their environment.

When people, conditions, and circumstances within which the association functions are fairly uniform, stable, and predictable, the association usually attempts to routinize certain decision-making processes by adopting sets of rules and regulations. For example, churches or missions receiving financial aid are required to meet specified requirements and to follow certain procedures. Tenure of office on boards, committees, and official elected positions may be limited in certain ways. New missions and churches can be established with associational blessing and support only if they follow prescribed procedures.

The development of rules and regulations, the precise specification of job responsibilities, et cetera, is commonly described as bureaucratization. In recent years bureaucratic organizations have been vigorously criticized (often justly) for being too inflexible, too slow to act, and too resistant to change and innovation. Many churches and associations have ignored such criticism, apparently feeling that the cost in effort, time, and money to change is such that demands for change can be ignored. Conservative leaders tend to feel that existing programs can be continued and meet the demands of the majority of those who make decisions about policy and support.

Bureaucratic rules and specifications seek to control extra-organizational influences that might prevent the smooth, efficient functioning of the organization. But what is often overlooked is that an organization humming along efficiently may be engaging in activities that make little real difference, that accomplish few ultimate objectives

43

for which the organization was established.

One needs to ask continuously not only about efficiency but also about effectiveness. Is the basic job of the association being accomplished through existing programs, activities, and procedures? In a rapidly changing environment, internal efficiency may need to be sacrificed for adaptability to increase effectiveness in meeting current needs. The nature of the specific task or problem confronting the association will determine the kind of organizational structure and policy utilized to deal with it.

For routine work the familiar rational, bureaucratic organizational structure may be both the most efficient and the most satisfying. Not all people can adjust easily to the hectic, open-ended, ad hoc, task force technique for dealing with associational and local church problems. It takes courage to be creative.

6. Levels Within the Associational Organization

Organization theorists identify three levels in most formal organizations: (1) the technical, (2) the managerial or administrative, and (3) the institutional or policy-making level. In a Baptist association the policy-making group would be the annual session and the executive board which functions temporarily on behalf of the whole association between annual sessions. They relate the association to the churches and other denominations and community groups. The administrative or managerial level is made up of the director of missions, the moderator, chairmen of major committees, church program organization directors, and other members of the associational council. The technical level consists of the host of volunteer workers and, in some cases, paid staff members who carry on associational programs, who produce many of the services the association was established to render. This level includes teachers of leadership training courses, consultants working with church leaders, youth revival teams, summer mission volunteers, and workers in associational day-care programs.

The association is one link in an entire system composed of churches, state Baptist conventions, and the Southern Baptist Convention, although each unit in the system is autonomous with respect to its own internal operations. For all levels of its work the association draws upon the personnel and financial resources of its affiliated churches. Individuals coming together from the various churches function and interact as interested Christians are expected to do, but each individual brings his total personality into the role the association asks him to fill. (See diagram at end of Chapter Two.)

7. Participation in Associational Work

To be an effective leader in associational work requires some understanding of how people work in groups, how their individual needs, goals, attitudes, and constraints motivate or restrict their participation in the work of the association.[24] Each individual usually is related to numerous other organizations, religious, civic, social, business, and political. The amount of time and energy any individual is prepared to devote to associational affairs will be dependent on individual priorities, the pressures from other groups both formal and informal to which he or she may be related, and the sense of urgency the individual feels regarding a particular program.

Although created and sustained by the participating churches, the association itself is a vital, adaptive organism, with many different parts or subgroups performing varied functions. The analogy of the human body which Paul used to describe the functioning of the church applies equally well to the association. It is constantly reacting and adapting to forces operating internally and to external forces in its environment (its community). If the association is to continue to enjoy the confidence and support of the participating churches and the individuals who function in any level of its work, it must maintain an acceptable level of performance of the work it was established to perform while at the same time satisfying the personal goals and needs of individual participants. The final section of Chapter Six offers suggestions to the association for evaluation and feedback.

Principles of Administration

8. The Association as a Voluntary, Autonomous Organization

The principle of freedom of association is built into the very fabric of American life. It is embedded in the Constitution of the United States and has been sustained by frequent decisions of the Supreme Court. This same precious principle of freedom and autonomy is built into Baptist polity.

Churches and associations have very permeable boundaries. It is relatively easy to get in and to get out. A church may choose to withdraw from the association and the association has no power to coerce continued relationship. Church members and others involved in associational activities are free to withdraw, to resign, or otherwise to disengage themselves from associational activities and groups. The association operates on the principle of persuasion and social pressures rather than coercion.

The association is a voluntary organization. There is no economic or political coercion requiring members to participate in its activities. As in most voluntary organizations, there is always a problem of maintaining membership participation and overcoming apathy. Often members in voluntary organizations are willing to leave the running of the organization to an active minority. Another problem frequently encountered is the attitude in contemporary society placing lower priority on church and associational obligations than on one's job obligations, civic club responsibilities, and other organizations with which one may be related.

Individuals and groups will be more interested and willing to work in associational programs when they see some relationship between their own personal, group, or local church goals and objectives with those of the association.

If the association is answering questions no longer being asked, if their meetings and programs seem irrelevant to the majority of church members, efforts should be made to make the association more responsive to pressing current problems. The pressure is on this generation of Baptist leaders to produce denominational systems, organizations, and procedures that work better than those inherited from the past. Society as a whole has come to expect more from its institutions. Particularly the young, the frustrated, and the powerless in society have been exerting increasing pressure upon the government, the schools, the churches, and other institutions of society, demanding that they live up to the ideals their leaders have so eloquently espoused. Many call for immediate action in areas where changes are slow. Dissatisfied with the pace of change, too many in the churches have become apathetic if not antagonistic toward any kind of denominational organization.

Associational leaders are closest to the church members geographically and philosophically. They can better discover and understand how the majority of church members feel about denominational organization and institute changes that will renew confidence in denominational programs and leaders.

9. Power and Control in Voluntary Organizations

Systems of authority, power and control are in church organizations just as they are in other types of organizations even though membership is on a voluntary basis. Etzioni identifies three kinds of power in organizations: 1. *Coercive power*—Resting on the application or the threat of application of physical sanction, generation of frustration, or control of the satisfaction of needs. 2. *Remunerative power*—Based on the allocation and manipulation of symbolic rewards, esteem, prestige, etc., exercised through persuasion, manipulation, or suggestions.[25]

For example, a church has more power over its ministers than over its members. The members are influenced by normative power, whereas the ministers are controlled by both normative and remunerative power and possibly by coercive power in the sense that frustration can be generated or the satisfaction of needs withheld. Similarly the association has more power over its paid staff members than over the church members who participate in associational activities or serve as messengers to the association. Commonly held beliefs, values, and norms act as constraints on the kind of behavior in associational activities which achieves group approval.

Principles of Administration

Associational leaders can help establish new "norms" and encourage new priorities for churches, groups and individuals. They accomplish this by education, persuasion, and suggestion, not by coercion. In the work of the association, changes are brought about not by coercion but through "a normative, reeducative" strategy which seeks to help people within the association to work out their own problems rather than to depend upon external groups to prescribe how things should be done. The *Associational Strategy Planning Guide* offers specific suggestions for discovering needs and implementing changes called for by local circumstances.

Power in the work of the association is the ability to induce or influence others to initiate, carry out, or stop a particular activity. Power involves the capability of causing a change in behavior. Power is earned on the basis of effective service rendered and is lost when not used properly.

Major changes in a church or an association require widespread support from the total membership. Many a new pastor has become frustrated over his inability to introduce improved procedures in the work of the church because of complacency of the church members. Replacing a few key leaders in an associational organization or providing specialized training for one or two key leaders may not bring about needed changes unless, through a process of reeducation, the values, objectives, and direction of the whole group can be changed.

Good intentions do not necessarily bring good results. When John F. Kennedy was elected President in 1960, he announced his intention to restore the State Department to its historic position as the major force for the conduct of United States foreign affairs. He established a special task force to study the problem and sought to appoint key administrators to revitalize the department. So great was the built-in resistance of the bureaucracy to change that within six months after his inauguration President Kennedy was saying that sending an instruction to the State Department was "like dropping it in the dead-letter box." [26]

48

The Association as Organization

10. The Association's Changing Environment

The association is shaped by its environment. Both the internal and external environment in which an association functions is continually changing. As we noted in Section 6 above, there are three component elements in an associational organization: (1) a policy-making, goal-setting group—the annual meeting and/or the executive board; (2) the administrators of associational work who monitor and direct; and (3) those responsible in the association for carrying out associational activities and operations.

Open systems depend upon feedback mechanisms to report the results of their activities. This feedback process supplies information constantly to the administrators internally to enable immediate adjustments to meet changing needs. Past mistakes are not repeated perpetually. New approaches using present organizational structures may be introduced. If present organizations and procedures are not sufficient, old structures may be supplemented or replaced by new organizational structures so that the association can respond appropriately to current and future needs. Open systems also provide for feedback from those outside the association to the policy-making group. This provides for continuing outside evaluation, feedback, and adjustments to keep the association "on target" in performing needed services to the churches, the community, the state, and national conventions of the denomination. This external feedback loop coming from the community is helpful in showing the response of the environment to the output of the associational organizational system. This feedback provides useful information for correcting policy and setting new goals.

The figure below diagrams the functioning of the system. The feedback loops A and B are crucial in assuring that the ongoing activities of the associations—its "product"—reflect the stated purposes of the association, which in turn should reflect the nature and mission of the church.

Principles of Administration

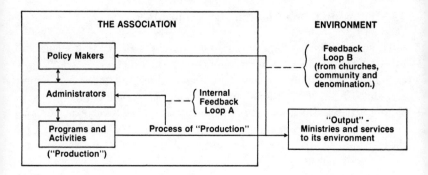

NOTES

1. James Daniel and Elaine Dickson, eds., *The 70's, Opportunities for Your Churches* (Nashville: Convention Press, 1969), pp. 136–138.

2. *Ibid.*, pp. 138–139.

3. See the *Associational Strategy Planning Guide* for help in this area; available from the Division of Associational Services, Home Mission Board. See also chapter five, section two, on planning.

4. Refer to chapter five, section one, on organizational processes.

5. Cf. Paul Hersey and Kenneth H. Blanchard, *The Management of Organizational Behavior: Utilizing Human Resources* (Englewood Cliffs: Prentice-Hall, 1972); and Eddy, William B., ed., *Behavioral Sciences and the Manager's Role* (Washington, D.C.: National Training Laboratories' Institute for Applied Behavioral Science, 1969).

6. Donal L. Metz, *New Congregations, Security and Mission in Conflict* (Philadelphia: Westminster Press, 1967), p. 135.

7. *Ibid.*, p. 145.

8. H. H. Gerth and C. Wright Mills, eds. and trans., "Bureaucracy," English translation in *From Max Weber, Essays in Sociology* (New York: Oxford University Press, 1946).

9. Warren G. Bennis and Philip E. Slater, *The Temporary Society* (New York:

The Association as Organization

Harper and Row, 1968), pp. 54–55.

10. *Ibid.*, p. 55

11. *Ibid.*, pp. 55–59.

12. Charles Perrow, *Organizational Analysis: A Sociological View* (Belmont: Brooks-Cole Publishing Company, 1970), p. 50.

13. *Ibid.*, p. 50

14 *Ibid.*, p. 50.

15. Morton F. Rose, Unpublished seminar paper, Southern Baptist Theological Seminary, Louisville, Kentucky, October 23, 1973.

16. Peter F. Rudge, *Ministry and Management* (New York: Barnes and Noble, 1970), p. 60.

17. Douglas McGregor, *The Human Side of Enterprise* (New York: McGraw-Hill, 1960), p. 33.

18. *Ibid.*, p. 43.

19. R. M. Cyert and J. G. March, *A Behavioral Theory of the Firm* (New Jersey: Prentice-Hall, 1963).

20. Amitai Etzioni, *Modern Organizations* (Englewood Cliffs: Prentice-Hall, 1964), p. 32.

21. Ludwig von Bertalanffy, *General System Theory: Foundations, Development, Applications* (New York: George Braziller, Inc., 1969). For further development of these concepts, see chapter six, "Systems of Change," in Warren G. Bennis, Kenneth D. Benne, and Robert Chin (New York: Holt, Rinehart and Winston, 1969), pp. 268–312.

22. Bennis & Slater, p. 98.

23. Charles Perrow, p. 56.

24. Recommended books for those desiring to improve their leadership skills include the following:

Gaines S. Dobbins, *Learning to Lead* (Nashville: Broadman Press, 1968).

William R. Cromer, *Introduction to Church Leadership* (Nashville: Convention Press, 1971)

Edward A. Buchanan, *Developing Leadership Skills* (Nashville: Convention Press, 1971).

25. Amitai Etzioni, *A Sociological Reader on Complex Organizations* (New York: Holt, Rinehart and Winston, 1969), pp. 59–60.

26. Arthur M. Schlesinger Jr., *A Thousand Days* (Boston: Houghton-Mifflin, 1965), pp. 407–447.

3.

Associational Administration

1. The Administrative Process

The following pages offer some suggestions, guidelines, principles, and concepts that may be useful to the director of missions, the moderator, program leaders, and many other associational leaders. The writer would emphasize that no statements of principles and procedures can, by themselves without the application of administrative skill and Christian concern, provide answers to administrative problems. No magic "administrative kit" exists that will provide practical rules to be applied automatically and mechanically to any and all administrative problems. Effective administration involves the internalization of some basic attitudes about persons, about the church—its nature and mission, about the association as an extension of the mission of the church, and about other denominational units and agencies.

Effective administration involves skills that have become thoroughly incorporated into the administrator's personality and life-style, not just skills acknowledged intellectually. Effective administration depends upon constant awareness of the changing environment in which the association functions. Such awareness requires thorough knowledge of the churches, of the other denominational organizations such as the state Baptist convention and the Southern Baptist Convention and its agencies. Knowledge of the social, economic, and political as well as religious forces at work in the community served by the association is essential.

Principles of Administration

The association exists to meet both internal and external needs. Good administration will see that the needs of participating churches and the denomination are being met, but also that effective ministries to the needs of the community and the world are being carried on.

Associations differ and the procedures in one association need not duplicate exactly the administrative procedures in another. One director of state missions asserted, "I'm convinced that there are, and probably should be, as many different associational programs as there are associations." Just as each church needs its own special structure, programs, and procedures suited to its unique set of circumstances, so the association will develop its own unique pattern without embarrassment that it does not duplicate procedures followed elsewhere. The important thing is that the association minister effectively to the unique needs of its community and its affiliated churches, utilizing the unique combination of resources available there.

Problems in associations arise from many sources. Some are people problems; some are leadership problems; some are due to organizational structure.

2. Approaches to the Study of Administration

In our study of the association as organization, we noted several different theoretical approaches to an understanding of organizations and an understanding of the most appropriate ways to administer them:

A. Some administrators, in describing their work for the benefit of others, have focused on the functions of the administrator or the steps in the administrative process. These are often described in precise bureaucratic policies and procedures.

B. The human relations theorists have been concerned with individual motivation and the application of psychology to the behavior of individuals in groups.

C. The open system theorists see administration as involving the interrelated social behaviors of all organizational participants and subgroups and their interaction with persons and groups outside the organization as well as within.

In studying any organization, some theorists focus on the important function of decision making by administrators. They seek to develop a dependable standardized process of analysis and decision making, noting the factors influencing one's perception of the problem, the alternative solutions open to the administrator, and the personal values against which he evaluates alternatives. Other scholars utilize mathematical models, taking advantage of the rapid calculating skills of the computer.

In studying associational administration, we should use whatever helpful insights may come from any of these approaches.

Within the Southern Baptist denomination, the recent era might be described as the era of the programmed church. Denominational agencies have clarified and codified their program assignments. Both denominational agencies and many churches have been involved in long-range planning. A new openness and freedom to make choices from several attractive options have created anxieties among many church and associational leaders more familiar with the carefully prescribed procedures and structures of the past. One responsibility of the association is to equip the churches for responsible freedom and choice.

3. Criteria for Acceptable Administrative Practices

J. C. Bradley has suggested three basic criteria for a theologically sound and practically effective system of administration. Administrative policies and actions should enhance (1) Christian maturity, (2) Christian community, and (3) Christian mission.[1] Bradley concluded that traditional administrative processes among Baptists had worked fairly well in achieving Christian mission; but when one views the vast number of church dropouts, the inactive church members, the turnover in volunteer workers each year, the demissions from the ministry, et cetera, it is apparent that present and past administrative processes have often failed in achieving Christian maturity and Christian community.

A major task of administration is the integration of personal and group goals of participants with the goals of the organization. Objectives and

Principles of Administration

goals of the association should be related directly to objectives and goals of the churches.

4. Administration Defined

The way in which one defines administration will depend in part on the particular theory of administration and organization which dominates one's thought and practice.

Simply stated, administration is working with and through people to accomplish organizational goals. It is an orderly way of assigning responsibility and guiding activity to accomplish objectives. Associational administration is the process of setting objectives and establishing policies, of creating and maintaining needed organizations, making plans and implementing them, evaluating results at each step, and making needed adjustments to assure the achievement of basic objectives.

Associational administration is an inclusive process, shared ideally by all participants in associational leadership. Administration is a legitimate, "spiritual" function. Wayne E. Oates has pointed to three New Testament concepts which "provide a profile for a religious meaning of administration."

> The first concept of administration in the New Testament is that of ministering. The Greek word for this is *diakoneo;* the literal meaning is "to wait upon others." . . . The second concept of administration is that of sharing in the corporate life. The Greek word for it is koinoneo; literally this means "distributing" charitably of one's goods, but more metaphorically it means communicating with others and forming a community of shared responsibility of its members for and with each other . . . . A third concept for administration in the New Testament is that of reflective observation and sustained attention to the total life of a people together. The Greek word for this is episkopeo; . . . . its more metaphorical meaning is "having good judgment, wide perspective, and the capacity to inspect, analyze, decide and oversee to completion a given set of relationships." The vertical dimension is that of "watching over the visitation of God to His people."

Oates summarizes these concepts:

56

Associational Administration

The administrator is an initiator who creates new possibilities in old forms. He is a perpetuator who sees to it that these are carried through to completion. He is a distributor who makes sure that both power and responsibility are shared by those who are subject to the decisions being effected. He is one who keeps his aim when others lose theirs. He maintains perspective of the totality of corporate relationships when other person's perspective becomes partial and segmented.[2]

Administration is a means of ministry, a way of guiding the processes of spiritual growth. Associational administration is an organized arrangement of interdependent systems in continuing interaction, rather than a checklist of separated, discrete actions, whether sequential or ongoing. The administrative process is carried on in the context of the total system, including all the forces at work in the individuals involved in the administrative process, the dynamics of the churches related to the association, and the pressures and concerns of other denominational agencies. It is useful, however, to study these separate functions or processes in administration as well as to seek an understanding of the characteristics of administration as a totality.

NOTES

1. J. C. Bradley, "A Transactional Theory of Church Administration" (Ed. D. diss., Southern Baptist Theological Seminary, Louisville, Kentucky, 1969), pp. 74–76.
2. Wayne E. Oates, *The Holy Spirit in Five Worlds* (New York: Association Press, 1968), pp. 96–97.

4.

Administrative Functions—Needs, Objectives, and Plans

In the next three chapters some functions or tasks involved in associational administration will be examined. Whatever one's role in the association—whether messenger or moderator, committee member or church program organization director, these steps in the administrative process are essential to effective work.

The first of these important steps is that of determining needs the association should seek to meet and deciding on priorities by setting worthy, clear, and attainable objectives.

I. Determining Needs and Objectives

Action is a response to a felt need. Apathy in associational work indicates deficiency in awareness of the real needs in the community and in the participating churches. Church members with knowledge of the nature and mission of the church, who participate personally in discovering the pressing spiritual needs of the community, will be more eager to assist the association in responding appropriately to those needs.

Denominational resources are available to aid in making surveys and locating problem areas, and to point to alternative programs and actions.

A. *The association exists to meet needs.* The only valid reason for the existence of an association is its ability to meet needs the churches could not meet as well without it. These needs may be individual, congregational, within or outside the Baptist fellowship, organizational, informational, or inspirational. Each association should provide for periodic review of the need in its area that it should seek to meet.

Watson [1] discusses several needs that each association may wish to explore to discover if any should be included in the list of needs it will attempt to meet in some way. These are needs for fellowship, communication, common understanding, motivation, information, ministry, strategy, a medium of cooperation, and church assistance. "The response of each association to any or all of these needs will be in proportion to the presence of the need, the recognition of the need by associational leaders, and the resources which are available to the association for meeting them." [2]

B. *Associational objectives and goals.* To understand any association fully, one must understand the objectives and goals it is pursuing. These provide the best single clue to the distinctive character of an association. But these objectives are often not written down. They may be as diverse as the number of participants in the work of the association. Indeed, some theorists insist that organizations do not have goals, that only people have goals. The author's conviction is that organization objectives and goals are more than the aggregate preferences of all participants.

Associational leaders will find the following pamphlets extremely helpful in the process of determining needs and objectives for the association. They are available from the Associational Administration Service Department of the Home Mission Board. The titles of the pamphlets are *Associational Strategy Planning Guide* and its companion piece, *Guide for Associational Self-Study.* The third pamphlet which should be used each year is *Annual Associational Planning Guide.*

We consider next some basic factors that should be kept in focus in the process of determining objectives and goals.

1. *Who shall determine objectives and goals?* Not every church member or participant in the association is equally involved in goal setting. Some individuals and groups are more vocal and/or more powerful than others in influencing the direction the organization will go. Cyert and March [3] describe goal setting in terms of the formation of

Needs, Objectives, and Plans

"dominant coalitions" among various individuals and groups in an organization, bargaining with others in an attempt to gain as many of their objectives as possible. Priorities reflected in the stated or operational goals of any organization usually represent a consensus of the objectives of several participant groups.

2. *Multiple goals.* Often agreement may not be complete within the association regarding its objectives and the priorities being observed. However, the association can function by acknowledging these multiple goals and by providng multiple programs to meet these varied and often conflicting objectives and goals of participating groups and individuals in the association. Those outside the association may hold objectives and goals for the association, such as community groups, agencies of the state convention or of the Southern Baptist Convention.

Organizational goals are multiple and may even be conflicting. The goal of a mother with a child in a day-care center sponsored by the association may be quite different from the goal of the associational treasurer. The goal of a youth choir member in an associational music festival may be quite different from that of the chairman of the associational personnel committee. These varying goals may be pursued in sequence or simultaneously. Indeed, the tension between conflicting goals may be a healthy stimulus to the association.

Organizational structures and leadership styles will vary with the goals being sought. To be "successful," associations do not have to have identical objectives, structures, schedules, or styles of leadership. Good associational administration will seek to insure internal consistency and harmony between the objectives of the organization and procedures utilized to achieve them. All will be selected in the light of their suitability for the particular time, place, and circumstance.

3. *Evaluation of objectives and goals.* Opportune times for the evaluation of its objectives come from associations doing long-range strategy planning, when they are making a change in their director of missions or other staff members, or at a time when a new association is being formed or two existing associations are being merged. Such an

evaluation should be regularly on the agenda of the associational council at the beginning and end of each associational year.

Albert McClellan has pointed out several dangers an association should avoid: 1. Duplicating structure and functions of the state conventions; 2. Organizing to meet the needs of state and Southern Baptist Convention agencies rather than to meet the needs of the churches; 3. Molding the associational program in the patterns of the past by continuing programs and structures not related to any denominational or church need (Example: the canned reports printed in associational minutes); 4. Attempting out-of-state mission programs.[4]

The association should not permit itself to be reduced to being merely a promotional agency for other denominational programs, particularly if this should cause the association to lose sight of its more fundamental reason for being, McClellan asserted. He urged that the association should stay as close as possible to its historic role, that it should place the emphasis at those points where it can be of most help to the churches. Its stance should always be toward the churches. He acknowledged the "lost motion" in many associations; conducting meetings that practically nobody attends, erecting organizations that do not function, employing underpaid assistants that add nothing except ego satisfaction to the director of missions, and conducting programs that do not meet the real needs of the churches. McClellan felt the associations have failed notably at two points: "(1) We do not create viable fellowships and (2) we do not discuss ways and means of applying Christian doctrine to the critical points of public action and attitude."[5]

McClellan urged associations to base their actions at the point of their strongest advantage—people-to-people contact. Ongoing programs that help the churches should have priority over special projects such as an annual barbecue. The association should generally avoid duplicating community services.[6]

We have stressed the significance of objectives and goals because the decisions made by associational leaders should be shaped by the objectives the association has set for itself. Objectives should determine the kind and amount of associational organization, the kind of leaders to be recruited and trained, the kind of resources that must be secured. Indeed, associational objectives may often supply the motive for participation. When goals are defined, participants and financial resources can often be mobilized around them.

The associational council or executive board may wish to utilize the material of this section to guide in a reevaluation of the objectives of the association and, if not stated in writing, lead the association to formulate and adopt a written statement of its objectives.

4. *Some proposed objectives.* Five objectives for the association are:

a. To provide for the spiritual welfare and fellowship of all the churches in the association
b. To provide a forum for the discussion of the Christian faith, the evaluation of denominational plans, policies, and proposals, and the evaluation of the doctrinal soundness of the churches cooperating with the association
c. To serve as a two-way channel of information and assistance between the churches and the state and Southern Baptist Convention and their agencies
d. To assist the churches in determining their own objectives and to aid the churches in planning, conducting, evaluating, and improving their programs of work designed to reach their objectives. The objectives of the association must be vitally related to the objectives of the churches.
e. To discover areas of spiritual need in its area and mobilize, coordinate, and channel the resources of the churches and of other denominational agencies either jointly or separately in meeting those needs.[7]

Watson listed the "functions" of the association as (1) to foster fellowship among the churches, (2) to foster unity in faith and practice, and (3) to provide assistance to churches.[8]

Effective administrators in each association will lead that association to study the needs in its area and determine its own objectives in the light of those needs. Suggestions for the achieving of each of these functions may be found in the *Associational Base Design.*

(1) To foster fellowship the association may provide means for congre-

gations and individuals to become better acquainted, to share in successes and failures, joys and concerns. By participating together in mission activities and other ministries, in leadership training, evangelism, social and recreational activities, members of the several churches in the association can become better acquainted and experience genuine Christian fellowship.

(2) To foster unity in faith and practice the association may provide in its general meetings forums for discussion of doctrinal, moral, social, and other types of issues important to people of the area. Doctrinal sermons followed by discussions, doctrinal courses included in leadership training schools, printed materials circulated by the association are some of the ways the association could be helpful.

(3) Upon request they may assist churches in examining candidates for ordination to the ministry, assist in constituting new churches, and offer counsel to churches experiencing problems.

Churches seeking affiliation with the association may receive counsel regarding the commonly held doctrinal positions of the churches which are currently members of the association. Associational leaders explore with the new congregations their understanding and acceptance of these basic doctrines forming the foundation for fellowship in the association. Such counsel and assistance from the association in advance will enable the credentials committee of the association to act with adequate information when messengers of the new congregation seek membership in the association.

The associations may discuss in various ways the issues and recommendations to be presented to the state Baptist conventions and the Southern Baptist Convention. Such discussions could prove to be valuable learning experiences for many Baptists now uninvolved in the shaping of denominational policies and programs at all levels. It could develop an informed constituency, better able to express themselves as messengers in the associations, state conventions, and the Southern Baptist Convention.

Five suggestions are offered for providing assistance to churches:

Needs, Objectives, and Plans

(a) Assistance from other Baptist bodies and other groups may be channeled through the association to the churches.

(b) The association may provide organization and leadership for cooperative projects through which the churches may provide assistance to themselves.

(c) The association may conduct for the churches the work they do to extend their own ministry cooperatively within the associational area.

(d) Associational leaders may provide personal assistance to individual churches upon request, and may assist in securing resources needed by individual churches.

(e) The association may lead churches to offer assistance to other churches, and the association may channel this assistance to the churches in need of it.[9]

II. Planning

Planning is the second of the ongoing administrative functions we shall seek to isolate and describe. Most organizational achievement flows from planned actions. In the beginning we should note that associational planning has certain built-in limitations. In suggesting careful planning we should not imply that the results of a given planned activity can always be known or controlled. As we noted in discussing the various views of organization systems, open systems such as Baptist associations in constant interaction with a changing environment must be flexible and adaptive, with constant evaluation and feedback to make course corrections in the direction of organizational work. The "system" in which an association operates contains more variables and uncertainties than any group of associational leaders can comprehend, predict, or control at any one time. The best laid plans of well-intentioned leaders have unintended consequences and are continuously affected by developments in other organizations and systems in the environment of the association. Therefore, plans must be continuously updated in response to the changing circumstances.

Organizations are more likely to succeed if they are "proactive" and not merely "reactive." Proactive associations review their needs and objectives and plan ahead for the detailed actions necessary to accomplish those specific objectives and goals. Reactive associations spend their energies dealing with whatever problem or crisis happens to arise.

A. *"An ounce of prevention is worth a pound of cure."* Planning will enable the association to initiate new programs as needed and to improve current operations. Planning begins with the determination of objectives; it sets priorities, chooses appropriate strategies, and outlines the preferred procedures for each of the contingencies anticipated.

Following the example of the early church as indicated in Acts, chapter 15, associational planning should provide for full participation of interested groups. Decisions reached by democratic procedures involve a balancing of interests that is usually fairer to all. The consensus also brings together varied perspectives in a view likely to be richer and deeper. Further, the motivation to work is increased by participation in planning.[10]

Long-term planning is usually initiated at the "policy making level" (cf. Chapter Two). Planning is done by the authority of the association itself or by the executive board. Staff work may be done by members of the board or assigned to paid staff personnel or others selected for planning responsibilities.

Annual planning done by the associational council is done by the authority of the programs assigned by the association. It is based on guidelines growing out of the associational objectives, purposes, and policies as determined by the association and/or its executive board. Each program organization or task force engages in technical planning for the ongoing work for which it is responsible.

Proper planning prevents poor performance.

B. *A plan for planning.* Let the associational leaders, whether staff, council, board, et cetera, visualize and describe in writing what the association should be like and what it should be doing five years in the future. Responses might be listed in such categories as what the association could mean to the pastors, to the churches, to the other denominational agencies, and to the community in which it exists. When these responses have been written down, list next the actions required to actualize the potentialities envisioned previously. What organization is required? What leadership is needed? What resources of funds and facilities are required? Write down next the reasons, if any, why the association is not functioning now as envisioned in the desired future. What are the causes of present difficulties? What are the forces for and against change? What resources do associational leaders offer to bring about desirable change?

Planning is simply a set of procedures by which an organization defines its goals and devises means to attain them.

The object of planning is to visualize the future of the organization in space and time. The longer the range of the planning projections, the more flexibility is needed to accommodate unforeseen events.

One critic of planning commented that, "It takes a real executive to leap from crisis to crisis but any fool can plan." That critic was overlooking the fact that effective executives use planning to prevent crises and to be better prepared to deal with the probable alternatives when they must leap from crisis to crisis. Planning can improve both efficiency and effectiveness.

C. *Planning through the associational council.* Planning in the association takes place at three levels: for the total association, at the program level, and at the unit level within each program. Time-wise, planning is done in three time frames: (1) long-range, (2) annual, and (3) event or project planning. The group responsible for overall annual planning is the associational council. Council members are more likely to be aware of the total needs and programs of the association and can, therefore, function most effectively in planning, correlation, and evaluation of associational work. Since the council is an advisory group, it will report its recommendations and plans to the executive board or the annual session of the association where the plans may be discussed, modified as needed, and adopted or rejected.

Event planning involves working out the details of activities, projects, or events that have been selected.

Principles of Administration

If a major revision of associational organizations and programs seems to be indicated, the association may wish, possibly upon the recommendation of the associational council, to establish a long-range planning committee to give extensive study to such reorganization. This committee of Baptist "decision makers" should include both lay persons and ministers, both men and women, both young and old, representing every major segment of the association.

D. *Resources for planning.* Associational administration Service Department of the Home Mission Board, *in cooperation with other SBC agencies* prepares an *Annual Associational Planning Guide.* This instrument will assist the associational council in identifying needs, determining priorities, setting goals, planning actions, assigning responsibility, reviewing and coordinating plans, allocating resources, promoting associational activities, and evaluating program achievements in the recommendations and reports that the council brings to the executive board or annual meeting. Copies are available upon request.

The council or the long-range planning committee of the association may find *Associational Strategy Planning Guide* helpful. This guide for long-range planning, is also available from this department. Other resources for planning which the council may find useful are listed in the *Annual Associational Planning Guide.*

E. *Responsibility for planning.* The primary job of the director of missions or other key leaders in the association is to see that planning takes place; not to do it himself. Why do we fail to plan? Lyle Schaller answers for the churches in a way that is equally applicable to Baptist associations.

> First of all, for almost all of the people who are a part of it, the (association) is a part-time item on the list of things they are thinking about. They are devoting a lot of their thinking time to other matters—whether they are housewives, businessmen, or farmers—where they *have* to plan ahead. The (association) is part-time also in that we have built in a pattern of leadership turnover so that even the person who is chairman of a key committee tends to see himself in a temporary role rather than a permanent role . . . Most

Needs, Objectives, and Plans

people are elected for only one year, and even though they may be re-elected year after year, there is a built-in assumption that it is only a one-year position. For example, the chairman of the finance committee will be thinking about this year's budget and next year's budget, and that's as far as he'll go because his term ends, so he doesn't think ahead.[11]

With rotating memberships on many committees and boards, it places great responsibility on the director of missions and the moderator to assume continuity in planning and implementation. This is not to suggest that they should enforce the plans of the past on a changing situation that calls for new approaches. Rather they should review the plans and update the programs and policies in light of changing circumstances. New leaders make possible new ministries, new approaches, new responses to previously unmet needs. The planning process works best when there is a built-in procedure for periodic review and feedback to assure course corrections.

F. *Time as a factor in planning.* Planning takes place in three time frames: (1) long-range planning, i.e., three to five years; (2) annual planning; and (3) operational planning which goes on quarterly, monthly, weekly, or even daily. The planning process should allow for (1) preparation time, (2) lead time, and (3) impact time.

Planners should look not only at the next step but also at the implications and probably reactions to taking that step. What alternatives are opened by taking that step and what alternatives are closed? An alternative that may appear immediately attractive may open a Pandora's box of later difficulties. For example, an association considering establishing an associational camp may discover that such a step would require far more money for construction, maintenance, and operation than the churches have been giving to all mission causes heretofore.

The association should plan in terms of the widely varied groups it attempts to serve. Schaller quoted the pastor of a large, Southwestern church who said that "when you're the pastor of a 3,000 or 4,000 member congregation you're not a shepherd, you're a rancher. And on a ranch you've got a lot of different herds, and you want to keep them all in their own separate pastures." [12]

The association on very rare occasions functions as a whole; more frequently as an aggregation of separate groups; and always in many of the same ways that other voluntary organizations function. A pastor may be related to a single Sunday School director while a director of missions must think and plan in terms of all the Sunday School directors in the association.

NOTES

1. E. C. Watson, *Associational Base Design* (Atlanta: Home Mission Board, 1972), pp. 51–65.

2. *Ibid.*, p. 65.

3. R. M. Cyert and J. G. March, *A Behavioral Theory of the Firm* (New Jersey: Prentice-Hall, 1963), p. 30.

4. Albert McClellan, "The Challenge of Associational Administration," (Unpublished address, February, 1970).

5. *Ibid.*

6. *Ibid.*

7. Report of *Conference on Associational Missions*, February 11–15, 1963, Gulfshore Baptist Assembly (Atlanta: Home Mission Board, 1963).

8. E. C. Watson, pp. 35–39.

9. *Ibid.*, pp. 38–39.

10. Arthur M. Adams, *Pastoral Administration* (Philadelphia: Westminster Press, 1964), p. 36.

11. Lyle E. Schaller, "The Anticipatory Style," *The Christian* Ministry, III, 3, May, 1972, 5ff.

12. *Ibid.*, p. 39.

5.

Administrative Functions— Organization and Leadership

1. Organizing the Structure, Programs and Relationships of the Association

A. *The process of organization.* If an engineer were employed to design a bridge across a stream, he would take several significant steps. He would learn something about the environmental constraints; the kind of rock or soil on which the foundations must rest, the amount of water expected in the stream, the wind currents, clearance required for river traffic under the bridge, et cetera. He must know what is expected of the bridge, the amount and kind of traffic. When all of his facts are assembled, he may then determine the various alternative designs capable of fulfilling the specified requirements. In light of the priorities and resources of the builders, the bridge may then be designed and built. If cost is the major conern, certain decisions will have to be made. If maximum safety, beauty, and environmental harmony or other factors have priority, then the designer will adjust his plans accordingly.

In designing an associational organization many of these same processes are useful. It is appropriate to raise such questions as the following:

1. What is expected of the association? Review the section on objectives. Survey the leaders and members in the affiliated churches, inquiring about what they would like the association to be and to do. The association is a vital link in a denominational system with expectations for

71

Principles of Administration

input and output. What services may the association legitimately perform for the state convention, the Southern Baptist Convention and its agencies? The association is linked to other community organizations—religious, moral, political, educational, social, et cetera. What organization on the part of the association is needed to equip it to respond to these various expectations?

2. What are the resources of the association? A young association made up of relatively new churches seeking to minister to a huge metropolitan center may find the needs and opportunities far greater than its available resources. Decisions must be made regarding priorities before establishing organization, employing paid staff members or enlisting volunteer leaders, and initiating new programs.

3. What organizational structure is appropriate and needed to achieve those objectives given priority by the association? How may the work be divided among the available people to achieve maximum results? How may tasks be delegated? How may standardized or normal procedures be developed so that repetitive tasks may be efficiently handled? What operational policies are needed and by whom shall they be developed?

Associational organization seeks an orderly and equitable grouping of responsibilities in order to achieve associational goals.

B. *Relating organization to needs and resources.* The San Jose Baptist Association in California has about the same number of churches, the same number of resident members, and some of the same spiritual goals as the Shelby County Baptist Association in Kentucky. Each association seeks to serve the needs of its community and its related churches. Yet when one contrasts the communities in which these two associations function he is made very much aware of how each association needs to structure its organization and program in terms of local needs and opportunities. The San Jose Association serves what some describe as the fastest growing metropolitan area in the United States. Ethnic groups from many parts of the world are found in the San Jose area, located at the south end of the San Francisco Bay. It is highly urbanized, secularized, affluent, and sophisticated, with a population of over one

72

Organization and Leadership

million. The Shelby County Association has one town of about 5,000 population and about 15,000 other people living in small towns, villages, and open country in a prosperous agricultural area.

About 6,000 Baptists in the twenty-four churches in the San Jose area are seeking to minister to fifty times the number of people as the 6,000 Baptists in twenty-four churches in the Shelby County Association.

Very obviously the kind of organization needed in San Jose is quite different from that indicated for a rural association. In still sharper contrast would be an association in a declining area where many churches are struggling to exist. Programs designed for the larger associations need to be simplified for the understaffed rural associations. Pastors working at secular jobs and giving only part-time service in church work will require a more streamlined program in the association if they are to participate. The association should continuously evaluate the kind and effectiveness of their organization in light of the stated or implied purposes of the association. Each association will need to respond to the program suggestions and organizational recommendations of state and Southern Baptist Convention agencies in light of its own needs, resources, and priorities.

C. *How much organization is needed?* It is said that someone once asked Abraham Lincoln how long a man's legs should be. Lincoln's answer was, "Long enough to reach the ground." How much organization does an association need? Only enough to get the job done. Proliferation of needless and unused organization is a waste of valuable time and energy and produces poor morale.

Several factors should be considered in shaping associational organization:

1. The nature and variety of problems in the area served by the association.
2. The geographical size, population density, transportation, and communication factors.
3. The socioeconomic, educational, and cultural levels in the area.
4. Work schedules of associational leaders and people in community

served.
5. The heritage from past associational history.
6. Changing emphases and cooperative patterns of other denominational agencies in state Baptist conventions and the Southern Baptist Convention. For example, in recent years many new Christian social ministry programs have been developed, often with three-way participation of the association, the state Baptist convention, and the Home Mission Board or some other denominational agency.
7. The number and kinds of groups in the community or at other denominational levels interacting or needing to interact in some way with the association.
8. The effectiveness and probable cost of various alternative plans.
9. The limitations and constraints indicated by community and denominational relationships.

D. *Ways of grouping activities and responsibilities.* In setting up associational organizations there are several ways of grouping the activities:
1. Geographically. Associations scattered over great distances or experiencing transportation or communications barriers may need an associational organization providing services in each of several geographic areas.
2. By church program organizations, i.e., Sunday School, Church Training, Woman's Missionary Union, Brotherhood, church music.
3. By age groups.
4. By emphases (evangelism, stewardship, mission action, et cetera.)
5. By types of services rendered, i.e., leadership training, camps and retreats, et cetera, or ministries performed to a particular clientele. When similar activities are grouped together the specialized knowledge and skill of leaders can be better utilized.
6. By the size or location of the churches.

Watson comments that "It is safe to conclude that when associations developed organization out of their sense of need, the organization was characterized by relevance, simplicity, and flexibility. When denominational pressure to conform became a prime motivation, the result often was organization that was complex, static, and sometimes unrelated to need sensed by associational leaders." [1]

Each association must weigh denominational recommendations against the local circumstances and choose the structure that is understandable and workable for the local personnel.

E. *Dealing with conflicting expectations.* Associational leaders are somewhat limited in what they will be able to do by the expectations of the association. To depart substantially from those expectations is to invite opposition or apathy. Leadership and authority become acceptable to a group when methods as well as goals represent prevailing attitudes and values.

Frequently the director of missions or any other associational leader may be confronted with competing and often conflicting expectations from different groups in the association. Some might desire the association to provide extensive audiovisual equipment and materials, while others insist on holding costs down. Some may be agitating for the purchase or construction of camp facilities far beyond the financial resources of the association, while others are encouraging greater support for the Cooperative Program.

The perceived importance and power of the groups making demands will govern what may be done, within the resources available. Often the groups may be ministered to sequentially rather than simultaneously so that there is a sense of staff members and other associational leaders equitably dividing their time among the several groups.

F. *Take account of the informal relationships existing in the association.* These informal liaisons can be useful and beneficial. They can be critical and destructive. The process of selecting associational leaders may not always bring to the formal positions of responsibility the most powerful leaders in the association. It is a wise administrator who quickly identifies the power structures in the community, the churches and the denomination, and thus will be able to inform, enlist support, and receive useful counsel from those with functional leadership in the community. Informal channels provide for rapid distribution of information. When utilized properly, such channels serve a very useful purpose. On the other hand such channels can be filled with rumors, misinterpretations of events, distortion of future plans, and other harmful gossip.

G. *Crises may necessitate and precipitate organizational change.* Stable communities enable associations to follow standardized patterns and develop uniform rules and policies for responding to predictable expectations. In areas of rapid growth or change, standardized procedures are not usable. In a heterogeneous and dynamic environment the association must organize to deal with contingencies and fluctuating needs and expectations.

It is evident in the New Testament record that churches of the first century developed and adapted organizational structures, practices and policies to meet the changing circumstances in which the churches sought to function. Christians in the twentieth century should be prepared to reform, reshape, or even reject whatever organizational structures are no longer viable as they find more effective ways of proclaiming the gospel, educating the believers, and ministering to their communities in the spirit of Christ.

H. *Accept the legitimacy and necessity of church and denominational organization.* We believe the church to have been divinely instituted and continually sustained by Jesus Christ, her founder and Lord. In this sense the church is a divine institution. The church and the association are composed of human individuals who behave in predictably human ways even though they may have been redeemed and transformed. Consequently, one might say that the church and denominational organizations which they establish are human organizations as well.

During the past decade there have been many critics of any form of organization in all areas of society. But if the antiestablishment critics should prevail to the point of dissolving all church and denominational organizations, churches would find it necessary immediately to devise

Organization and Leadership

new organizational structures and relationships to have any possibility of doing the work committed to them by the Lord Jesus Christ.

Men form organizations and adopt procedural policies in order to have an effective, standardized way of dealing with repetitive decisions. Organizations establish dependable and enduring relationships and routinize procedural behavior in order for members and leaders to concentrate on the really significant issues and decisions. A structureless community, without formal organizations to perform many of its tasks, would be as unusual, if not as impossible as an ocean without water. Unfortunately, it is characteristic of many organizations to shift their focus and concern from ends to means, neglecting the original and basic reason for existence in preoccupation with the machinery of organizational maintenance.

If leaders of the association can remember the basic reason for the existence of the association, they will be better able to adapt frequently as circumstances change. The problem faced in church and denominational life is the pervasive human temptation to canonize as essential or even as sacred the organizational relationships that were developed to meet needs of a past era but that are no longer responsive to needs of the present.

I. *Plan for and practice participatory democracy.* We have long given lip service to the doctrine of the priesthood of all believers. It is time to put it into practice in denominational administration. Because of what we believe about soul competency, the integrity and worth of each individual, because of the increasing complexity of contemporary society, associations need to enlist a wide spectrum of leadership skills from both laity and clergy. The needs confronting most associations are so diverse and human resources available in this age of specialization are often so varied, that the association faces the challenge of bringing the two together. In this era no single individual or even a small group of individuals, however dedicated and talented, can be expected to have either all the information or professional skills to respond to the total needs of the community, the churches, the individual church members

Principles of Administration

with all their varied problems and possibilities.

Discovering needs, determining priorities, planning programs and actions, ministering, teaching, counseling and guiding are all activities in which the widest possible participation should be sought. The director of missions, the moderator, or other associational leaders function best not as decision makers for the group but as enablers, pointing out possible alternatives, raising questions, sharing information about possible resources, and otherwise helping each group and each organization within the association to structure its organization and plan its activities to achieve basic objectives. The association should choose as its leaders those who have clear insights into the values and objectives the association is pursuing, who are able to ask penetrating questions about how successful the association is in pursuing its stated objectives.

The effective leader in a Baptist democracy will maintain a clear vision of the purpose of the organization and will help those he leads to look beyond their ongoing activities to think of their relation to the achievement of associational objectives. The associational leader in his own vision and enthusiasm will incarnate the purposes and values of the association.

Everyone whose cooperation is necessary to the successful implementation of a decision should be consulted in the making of the decision. Those closest to any problem are likely to have the most concrete understanding of the real nature of the problem. The membership in any organization is more likely to consent to and support decisions they helped to make. Participants consider themselves more bound by decisions of their own making and work diligently to achieve goals they helped to set, much more than for decisions and goals imposed from above. In denominational life, as in the political world, the authority of government rests on the consent of the governed. Participatory democracy both in planning and implementation is best to assure the best possible information inputs into the decisions and goals being set and to secure the best possible cooperation with the outcome or implementation of those decisions.

Organization and Leadership

J. *Keep the organization simple.* Only essential organization units should be established. If there is not enough work to be done to justify a permanent organization, ad hoc committees or task forces should be set up for particular assignments and then be dismissed when their work is completed.

K. *Patterns of associational organization.* Each association is, of course, free to decide for itself the pattern of associational organization that best fits its needs and resources. Suggestions given here are designed to aid leaders in finding effective structures and procedures, rather than to prescribe any given organizational pattern.

E. C. Watson, Morton Rose, and Loyd Corder, in developing the *Associational Base Design* for the Inter-Agency Council, offered four alternate patterns. One is a very simple plan for the very small, scattered association with limited personnel and resources. Other plans are for associations of increasing size and resources.

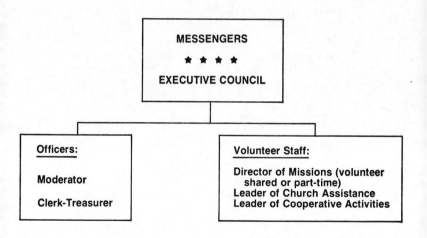

Principles of Administration

Pattern A is proposed for small associations with limited resources. It combines the executive board with the associational council into a single "executive council," whose members include the moderator, the clerk-treasurer, and volunteer staff members. No standing committees are suggested since the executive council can perform committee functions. Ad hoc committees or temporary task forces may be created as circumstances require. No church program organizations are included in Pattern A.

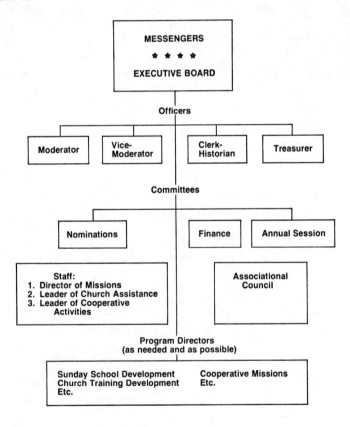

Organization and Leadership

Watson, et al, suggests Pattern B for small associations with limited resources, but where a nontraditional approach to organization is desired." (p. 136) As noted, it suggests only three standing committees. Ad hoc (temporary) committees would be named as needed for such functions as credentials, resolutions, properties, personnel, and camp. The Annual Session Committee could include in its work the work of the credentials committee as well as work usually done by committees on order of business and time, place, and preacher. Program directors should be selected for those areas where they are especially needed and available. Where program directors are not available, the three suggested staff members, whether paid or volunteer, would provide leadership.

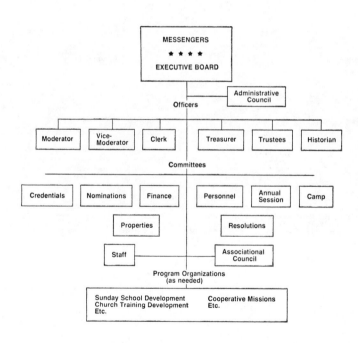

Principles of Administration

Pattern C is "suggested for associations for which the resources and opportunities require a more expanded type of organization." Note that a credentials committee, trustees, and a properties committee have been added.

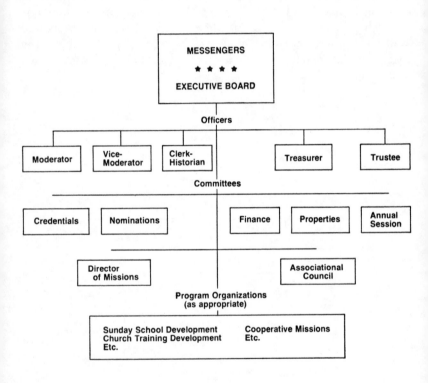

Organization and Leadership

Pattern D is designed for large associations with more ample resources. Note that some committees have been added and an administrative council is suggested to review administrative policies and procedures as needed.

L. *Organizing and reorganizing an association.* In areas where the Baptist population is growing, new associations may better meet the needs of the community and the churches. In areas where population is declining, existing associations may need to be merged in order to have a viable, healthy fellowship and to provide more adequate resources for needed ministries. Initiatives for merger may be taken within any association involved. The first step may well be requesting neighboring associations to join in forming a study committee to explore various possibilities. The state missions director may be asked to serve as consultant or as temporary chairman while plans for possible new associational organizations are being made.

Even when existing associations remain intact, cooperative relationships with neighboring associations in the employment of a director of missions or other staff members are often advisable.

M. *Messengers and their functions.* The official constituent members of associations are the messengers elected by the churches affiliated with the association according to the plan of each church. The associational constitution and bylaws normally prescribe the number of messengers each church may send. A typical provision is for each church to elect three messengers for the first one hundred members and one additional messenger for each additional one hundred members up to a maximum of ten.

It is recommended that each messenger serve for a full year, representing the church at each meeting of the association. Several associations hold two sessions annually, some more. It is recommended that the association have two business sessions per year, one in the spring for the election of officers and one in the fall for annual reports. Each church should give its messengers an opportunity to make an oral report to the congregation following the associational meetings.

Principles of Administration

N. *Executive board.* Except in small associations using Pattern A organization, associations elect annually an executive board consisting of two or more persons from each church, preferably from among the messengers named by the churches. Some associations request the churches to nominate their executive board representatives to be elected by the association. Ex officio members of the executive board serve by virtue of election to certain associational offices. Usually the pastor of each church is selected as an executive board member. Other members may serve on a three-year term, with one third of the lay board members' terms expiring each year. The executive board may meet monthly, bimonthly, quarterly, or more often if circumstances require. Normally, officers and committees of the association function also as the officers and committees of the board.

The executive board serves as the association ad interim, implementing policies adopted by the association, and carrying forward the administration of the work of the association observing such limits as may be imposed by the association's constitution and bylaws.

The association may assign to the executive board responsibility for making plans, preparing budgets, scheduling associational activities, administering personnel policies and all other matters related to the effective performance of the work of the association. Helpful pamphlets are available from the Associational Administration Service Department of the Home Mission Board.

O. *Responsibilities of associational officers.* (The following recommendations are drawn largely from the Associational Base Design.) [2]

Although the association elects officers annually, it should be understood that many officers may be reelected to give continuity and stability to the work of the association.

1. Moderator: It is suggested that the moderator be recommended by the nominating committee and elected by the association for a one-year term with the possibility of serving a second one-year term. Specific provision should be included in the constitution and bylaws for this and other officers.

Organization and Leadership

The moderator is responsible for conducting the sessions of the association and the executive board in proper parliamentary form. It is recommended that he study carefully *Robert's Rules of Order, Newly Revised,* or whatever other parliamentary manual the association may have chosen. He should consult with the director of missions and appropriate committees in formulating the agenda of executive board meetings and of the association. Through the executive board, and other channels, he shall coordinate the work of the association and its officers and committees. Upon request of the association or its executive board, he may assume the duties of the director of missions when the association is not served by one.

2. Vice-Moderator: The vice-moderator should be chosen by the same process as the moderator. His principal function is to assist the moderator in the performance of his duties and to perform other services as requested by the association or its executive board.

3. Clerk: The clerk is elected by the association upon the recommendation of the nominating committee. He may succeed himself. An assistant clerk may also be chosen in the same manner when the work load demands. The clerk records and keeps in legible, permanent form all transactions of the association and its executive board and, when requested, of the associational council. The clerk is a key person in the gathering of denominational information. His responsibility is to distribute the forms for the annual letter from the churches and secure these reports from the churches, send the statistical reports to the state convention and Southern Baptist Convention offices, and prepare a report for the association. The clerk will handle official associational correspondence, and collect, process, distribute, and interpret associational records as requested. The clerk will work with the historian in making available the records and archival materials concerning the history of the association. He will supervise the preparation of the annual minute of the association and distribute the minutes to the churches and other interested agencies and libraries. The clerk will assist the annual session committee in the registration of messengers at associational sessions,

checking registrations with the lists of messengers reported on the church letters to the association. He will notify in writing all officers and committees of their election and will keep in the permanent files of the association the minutes of associational committees. He will assume the responsibilities of associational historian when the association has none.

4. Treasurer: The treasurer should be elected by the association upon the recommendation of the nominating committee for a one-year term with the provision that he may succeed himself in office. He reports to the association and its executive board on all financial matters of the association. With the assistance of the finance committee he receives, deposits, disburses, and renders a faithful accounting of all associational funds. He should be bonded to give full assurance regarding financial security and integrity. The treasurer posts records of the contributions of each church and other contributors and reports at least quarterly upon all receipts and disbursements.

After examining supporting data for all check requests the treasurer will issue checks, cosigned when required.

5. Trustees: Three trustees should be elected by the association upon the recommendation of the nominating committee, one each year for a three-year term. As indicated in Patterns A and B the trustees may be any designated officers of the association, serving ex officio. Trustees act as legal agents of the association in the handling of property and other specified business matters as directed by the association.

6. Historian: The associational historian, elected annually upon the recommendation of the nominating committee, gathers and preserves historical records and materials related to the life and work of the association.

P. *Responsibilities of associational committees.* All committees should be elected by the association upon the recommendation of the nominating committee. Depending upon the size of the association, committees should consist of three to nine members, elected for three-year terms on a rotating basis with one third of the committee being elected each year. The executive council or executive board should recommend to the association the committees needed and their size. Each committee should select its own chairman and secretary or the chairman may be designated by the nominating committee and approved by the association. Frequency of meeting would be determined by the work to be done. Reports may be made to the association or the executive board. Free pamphlets on the work of these committees are available to associational leaders from the Associational Administration Service Department of the Home Mission Board.

1. Credentials Committee: The credentials committee will assist the association in determining when churches are of like faith and order and can be properly accepted or continued in the associational fellowship. They will counsel with churches seeking admission to the fellowship of the association and will examine the credentials of such churches in matters such as doctrine and practice, bringing a recommendation to the association regarding the seating of messengers from such petitioning churches. They shall examine, as requested by the association, any reported irregularities in the churches which may threaten their continued fellowship in the association.

2. Nominating Committee: The nominating committee selects, interviews, and enlists general associational officers (other than staff members), program organization leaders, and committee members and brings its recommendations to the association or its executive board. They shall assist program leaders in discovering and enlisting qualified leaders for their respective organizations and approve such workers before they are invited to work in the organizations.

3. Finance Committee: The finance committee will assist the association in securing, administering and reporting its finances. They shall develop and recommend to the association an overall stewardship development plan, an associational budget, policies, and procedures for financial management. They shall review expenditures periodically in terms of budget allocations and recommend budget adjustments as

needed to the association or its executive board.

4. Properties Committee: The properties committee shall assist the association in matters related to property administration. At least annually they shall inspect and inventory associational properties. They shall recommend to the personnel committee the employment, training, and supervision of custodial and maintenance personnel. In consultation with the staff supervisor they shall develop scheduled cleaning and maintenance procedures for associational facilities and equipment. They shall develop and recommend to the association an adequate insurance plan to protect the association and its properties.

5. Personnel Committee: The personnel committee shall assist the association in paid and volunteer staff personnel administration. They shall periodically survey the needs for associational staff positions, prepare or revise position descriptions for all staff personnel, and bring recommendations to the association or its executive board regarding the employment of personnel after careful interviews and consultation with appropriate supervisors. They shall prepare and maintain an organizational manual indicating relationships, policies and procedures for associational employees and volunteer staff members. They shall develop and recommend salary schedules and benefit programs for associational employees.

6. Annual Session Committee: This committee shall assist the association in planning and conducting the sessions of the association. Their duties shall include those previously performed by the committee on order of business and the time, place, and preacher committee. They shall propose to the executive board an order of business for the sessions of the association and enlist the personnel as required. They shall publicize to churches, state convention leaders, and the general public, information about the program. After consultation with the moderator and staff and program personnel, they shall arrange for facilities needed for the associational sessions. In consultation with the clerk they shall arrange for and conduct registration of messengers and visitors at the sessions. They shall receive in advance of and/or during the sessions

invitations from churches to future annual meetings and suggestions regarding speakers for the associational sessions and shall propose at each annual session the meeting place(s) and preacher(s) for the next year.

7. Camp Committee: This committee shall assist the association in matters relating to the administration of a camp program as a service to the programs of the association. Where the need justifies and the resources of the association are adequate, this may involve the securing, through purchase, construction, lease, or rental of camp facilities in consultation with the trustees and properties committees. They shall recruit, interview, and recommend to the personnel committee, in consultation with the director of missions, the employed and volunteer staff for the operation of any associational camp program. They shall recommend a budget for the association's camp program and administer such a budget when approved. They shall plan and recommend to the association a program of maintenance and improvement of camp property. They shall work with the associational council in planning the schedule and supervising the operation of the camp and the use of the camp facilities by others. They shall make these facilities available to churches and other groups in accordance with plans approved by the association. They shall consult with the finance and properties committee to assure that adequate insurance protection is provided for both property and liability risks.

8. Resolutions Committee: This committee shall assist the association in studying resolutions and bringing recommendations for resolutions to be adopted by the association. They shall receive, review, and recommend as they determine appropriate resolutions or public statements on behalf of the association. They may initiate resolutions or statements for the association or the executive board to consider.

Q. *Associational constitution and bylaws.* Every association should adopt and revise as needed a constitution and bylaws, setting forth the nature, relationships, membership, officers, boards, and committees of the association. A statement of faith, developed by the association or adopted from other sources such as the 1963 Statement of Faith adopted by the Southern Baptist Convention, may be included in the constitution or adopted as a separate document. The constitution sets forth the basic structure and purpose of the association. The bylaws contain details of implementation and procedures that are subject to more frequent changes.

S. F. Dowis in the *Associational Guidebook* [3] suggested eleven items to be included in the constitution:

  (1) Name
  (2) Purpose
  (3) Membership
  (4) Articles of Faith
  (5) Officers
  (6) Authority
  (7) Organizations
  (8) Executive Board
  (9) Meetings
 (10) Committees
 (11) Amendments

Bylaws should specify the parliamentary authority (usually *Robert's Rules of Order, Newly Revised*), the procedure for the election of officers and committees, and the employment of staff members.

R. *Incorporating the association.* There are many values in officially incorporating the association. State laws regulating the procedures for incorporation vary from state to state. Information can usually be obtained by writing to the secretary of state in the state capitol or by consulting a competent attorney who can assist in preparing the necessary papers. By incorporation the association gains legal status and continuity. It is able to own property and conduct business affairs in its own name. Officers of the association are not then personally liable for acts of the corporation.

S. *Policies and procedures manual.* Some larger associations with numerous staff members, programs, property, and activities find it useful to prepare and maintain a policies and procedures manual setting forth procedures for the various activities of the association, such as employment and benefit policies, purchasing and budget control policies, reporting procedures and forms. A description of the responsibilities of the officers, committees, executive board, and staff members and the procedures to be followed in their work may be included in such a manual. Policies with respect to the use of associational camp facilities, equipment, et cetera, may be included. By routinizing certain repetitive decisions and stating them as operational procedures, valuable time in committee and board meetings can be given to basic matters relating to objectives rather than to petty operational details.

2. Enlisting, Training, and Utilizing Human Resources

Associations accomplish their work with and through people, the leaders, and members drawn from the participating churches. We have considered earlier the determination of needs and priorities, the decisions that need to be made about organizational structure required to achieve the desired objectives.

In this section we focus on the procedures for enlisting, training, and utilizing fully the human resources related to the work of the association. We look first at the wider constituency of the association, the affiliated churches with all their members.

A. *Qualifications of affiliating churches.* Each association determines for itself the qualifications it expects of churches seeking affiliation. The association is free, under the leadership of the Holy Spirit, to accept or reject those churches meeting or failing to meet such qualifications. Each church is also free to determine whether it shall seek or maintain fellowship with the association. Churches received into the fellowship of the association are expected to be of like faith and order with the churches constituting the association, sympathetic with its purposes and programs, and cooperative in spirit.

A church desiring to be related to the association should consult with the credentials committee, the moderator, and the director of missions. They should explore together the doctrines, policies, and practices of the petitioning church and of the association. The credentials committee should be prepared to make a recommendation to the association regarding the seating of messengers from the petitioning church, thus welcoming them into the associational fellowship. In voting to receive a new church the association assumes a serious responsibility for providing genuine Christian fellowship and assistance to the new church and all its members. The new congregation should be fully informed of the many services provided by the association and the ways in which they, too, through the association, may become involved in ministry, mission, and church program development. Procedures for the selection of messengers annually, of sharing the financial support of the work of the association, and ways of participating in the various programs of the association should be communicated to all affiliating churches.

B. *Selecting associational leaders.* The director of missions and other paid or volunteer staff members will be discussed in a subsequent chapter. We focus now on the officers of the association and its board, committees, and program organizations. These leaders are needed to help the association maintain itself and function effectively in meeting needs of the churches.

Leaders should be selected from among the dedicated and competent church members who have an interest in and a willingness to learn more about helping churches and individuals and render Christian ministries to those in the community. Those who have demonstrated leadership ability and faithfulness in their own churches are most likely to be effective associational leaders.

The associational nominating committee plays an important role in the discovery and enlistment of leaders. They will depend largely on the recommendations of pastors, program leaders, and other leaders from the local churches to identify those with ability and other qualifications for associational leadership. After agreeing upon an individual for a leadership position, the nominating committee shall contact that person to secure his or her consent to serve if elected. Workers in the program organizations of the association shall be recommended to the nominating committee by the program leaders, who will then contact such workers after approval by the nominating committee. The constitution and bylaws should provide for the election of key leaders by the executive board so that these leaders may complete plans for the year and aid in the enlistment of other workers. Elections should be far enough in advance for officers to share in state convention emphasis training conferences before the new year begins.

C. *Inducting and orienting leaders.* New leaders should be recognized in the associational session or the executive board; information should be distributed to the churches through the associational newsletter. Program organization workers should be recognized and inducted appropriately into the meetings of the program organizations. The moderator, committee chairmen, and the director of missions all share in the responsibility for helping new and continuing leaders understand the basic objectives of the association and the contribution their work will make to achieving those objectives. Procedures, methods of work, reporting arrangements, and resources available for accomplishing the work should all be communicated each year to the associational leaders. Ideally the new leadership team should review the objectives and evaluate the procedures, the strengths, and weaknesses of existing programs, etc., as a prelude to setting new goals for the coming year. Existing policy and procedure manuals should be distributed, discussed, and revised as necessary in light of changing circumstances and leadership personnel.

The director of missions and moderator should insure that adequate leadership training opportunities are provided, either locally or in state or national conferences, so that associational leaders are as well trained as resources make possible, in performing the tasks they have been elected by the association to do.

Apathy and lethargy in associational work may reflect inadequate understanding of the purpose and potential of the association. Widespread participation in decision making helps to overcome the feeling of not being really involved. When associational affairs are controlled by a small minority, participation and interest quickly drop. Business sessions which "rubber stamp" decisions made elsewhere offer little of interest or value to the constituency, whose support and involvement are very much needed.

NOTES

1. E. C. Watson, *Associational Base Design* (Atlanta: Home Mission Board, 1972), pp. 123–124.

2. The following recommendations are drawn largely from the *Associational Base Design*.

3. S. F. Dowis, *Associational Guidebook* (Nashville: Convention Press, 1959), pp. 128–131.

6.

Administrative Functions— Directing, Coordinating, Communicating, Financing, and Evaluating

We continue in this chapter a study of five additional steps in the administrative process.

1. Directing Associational Work

The previous steps that have been discussed in the administrative process are important, yes, even essential; yet, they are only preparatory to achieving the work for which the association exists. Many fine plans and elaborate organizations never bear fruit, because no one assumes responsibility for directing the necessary work to achieve the designed objectives.

A. *Decision making.* Directing involves a number of interdependent activities. In all of these activities the process of decision making is important. Getting decisions made by the right people at the right time and in the right direction is at the heart of the administrative process. Associational work involves decisions of many types, being made continuously, about the use of time, resources, facilities, priorities, and personnel.

In making decisions individually or as a group, the first step is to define the problem. What kind of problem is it? What is its critical factor? When does the problem need to be solved? What will it cost to solve it? Expectations should be defined. What does the group wish to gain or attain by solving the problem?

Principles of Administration

The next step is to consider alternative solutions. It may be possible to anticipate which of several alternative solutions offers the surest way of achieving the desired goal and avoiding undesirable, unexpected consequences.

The administrator will need to know what to do with a decision after it has been reached. He is responsible for seeing that decisions reached by various groups in the association are properly implemented.

There are some common pitfalls in the decision-making process. Some groups waste extraordinary amounts of time and energy finding answers for the wrong problems. Others make the mistake of making decisions at the wrong time. Some are postponed that should be made immediately. Others are made long before they should be, before the decisions are really necessary. Another common mistake is making decisions that do not result in actions. A decision without a definite action plan and without adequate control of its execution is not an effective or even a finished decision.

When should associational leaders make decisions? Ray Johns makes four helpful suggestions which have been adapted and applied to associational work:

1. Make decisions when consensus points are reached. After possible choices have been discussed thoroughly by everyone concerned, after all available facts have been examined and possible reactions and results have been considered, points of agreement can usually be reached. Associational leaders can acquire the ability to recognize such areas of agreement. Promptness in reaching decisions will free groups to concentrate on more difficult problems.
2. Make decisions when emergencies require action. Critical situations sometimes develop which require decision and action even though all desired acts are not available. Associational leaders must have the capacity and courage to act on the best available data and to be able to live with the consequences.
3. Make decisions when obsolescence threatens. When programs, services, ministries, personnel, or facilities are out of date and ineffective, they endanger the stability and usefulness and possibly the very life of the

Other Administrative Functions

association. Associational leaders are responsible for initiating processes to bring about change and leading the association to make the necessary changes.

4. Make decisions before action is needed. Early consideration of questions well ahead of the time when action will be required gives time for consideration and discussion without pressure or strain and will prepare the people for changes when the time comes for them to be made.[1]

B. *Delegating responsibility and authority.* A significant step in effective administration is the delegation of responsibility and authority to those within the organization. The annual meeting should delegate certain responsibilities to its officers, executive board, and committees. Workers within the association need to know clearly what decisions they are expected to make themselves, what must be brought back to committees, boards, or administrators, and what actions are outside the realm of their responsibility. This information should be clearly communicated at the time leaders are elected to office.

An administrator, whatever his associational office, who has to have the final word on everything, who is incapable or unwilling to delegate responsibility, prevents the association from functioning effectively and prevents all of those who are working with him from growing to their full potential as spiritual leaders. The democratic leader will trust his associates; he will remain close enough to them to know when they need help but will encourage each individual and each group to make its own decisions.

The effective associational administrator will develop skill in initiating action in order to get programs and projects under way once decisions have been reached.

Effective administrators will seek to make maximum use of the individual differences and wide variety of competences that exist within the association. Effective leaders will welcome those with creative ideas and give them an opportunity to present their points of view. The leader will seek to maintain a responsible balance between authority and freedom.

C. *Directing democratically.* The associational leader will seek to keep the administrative processes democratic. In a democratic organization the objectives, plans, and policies will be determined by the group. The varied abilities and experience of participants are valued and utilized. Individual potentialities are continually enhanced so that associational goals are being realized with a maximum use of shared creative power and a minimum of human friction. There should be periodic, critical, and cooperative evaluation of methods and procedures, of goals and aims as well as of results.

The following principles for achieving democratic staff relationships have been adapted from Ray Johns [2] and applied to associational work:

1. *A respect for and acceptance of persons is fundamental.* An administrator encourages respect for others by the way in which he deals with everyone in the organization regardless of their status or background. If he actually believes in the dignity and worth of all individuals, regardless of economic or social position or race, creed or color, his behavior will have a part in establishing policies and procedures and relationships consistent with such a concept among all persons in the association.

2. *A sense of mutuality and confidence is necessary.* An executive must demonstrate in day-to-day relationships his confidence in those with whom he works. He must develop skill in showing how he can learn from others, how he depends on others, if they are to contribute fully to the relationships involved. He must learn to involve others in decision making.

3. *An atmosphere conducive to self-expression and relaxed relationships is essential.* The director of missions, the moderator, and other administrators can help in developing such an atmosphere. Other staff members have to be encouraged to express their attitudes or points of view. Administrators, sometimes quite unintentionally, discourage the expression of differences of opinion. Sometimes nonconformity is penalized. Administrators need to delay stating their opinion and on occasion to elicit first the viewpoint of other staff members or committee members.

Other Administrative Functions

4. *Freedom from fear, insecurity and frustration underlie coopera-tive, democratic relationships.* Administrators can help by assuring equitable policies regarding tenure of employment, by establishing con-ditions for satisfying personal relationships, and by eliminating causes of tensions among employees of the association.

5. *Equity in work loads and responsibilities are also necessary.* Some staff members must be encouraged to limit their work schedules; others must be stimulated to add to them or to keep them focused on the objectives of the association. The director of missions should not claim or accept special privileges for himself not available to other staff members unless they are clearly necessary to carry out his special responsibilities.

6. *Use of the group process in planning and decision making is one of the major ways by which democratic relationships are established.* As the chief administrator uses the group process he will teach and encourage others to do so.

7. *A sense of discipline, of mutual responsibility and accountability, must at the same time be developed.* Cooperative relationships must be responsible relationships. If people are to be free to choose, to help make decisions, they must accept a degree of responsibility for imple-menting decisions and for the results.

8. *A sense of wholeness and of responsibility for the total enterprise is important.* All need to be aware of how one part of the associational organization is related to other parts and the way in which their work contributes to these ends democratically chosen by the association.

9. *The integration of personal goals and associational purposes is fundamental to democratic relationships.* The director of missions and other associational leaders can help staff members and participants in associational organizations to integrate their personal goals with the goals of the association.

2. Coordination

Another process in effective administration is that of coordination, which seeks to develop a smooth interplay of the different component parts of the association, so that its purposes will be realized with a minimum of friction and maximum of collaborative effectiveness.

The executive board and associational council are major instruments to facilitate coordination in the association. Through the council and the executive board the director of missions and other leaders will seek to coordinate all the varied activities of the association into one harmonious program of work. Coordination is bringing individual effort into harmony with group goals. It is the integrating of efforts of subsystems with efforts of the whole system.

Coordination is best achieved in the early stages of planning and decision making. When planning is taking place, whether in the staff, the council, or the board, there should be continuing opportunity for coordination and evaluation. Coordination is useful in avoiding overlapping and duplication, in conserving available resources and energy, and in directing available energy and resources toward the achievement of associational objectives and goals.

3. Internal and External Communication

A. *The association as communication center*. Every association needs a central office for collecting, processing, and storing information, from which information may be distributed to various groups and individuals. The associational office should serve as this records center.

Effective associational administration requires open and well-used channels of communication both to the internal public (associational leaders and members and leaders of churches affiliated with the association) and the external public (including other Baptist organizations, religious groups of other denominations, civic, political, social, and educational groups).

Each participant in the associational organization team needs to be aware of what is going on elsewhere in the association and the churches and also to see the relationship of the work they are doing to what is being done by others. In its external relationships with state conventions and Southern Baptist agencies, the association is not merely a pipeline or funnel to pass along information and instructions from these denominational groups to the workers in the churches. Communication should be multidirectional, with the association involved in gathering information from the churches and the community and transmitting it on to relevant groups both within their own structure and to those outside.

The association serves as the nerve center of a communications network with information flowing in all directions. Some of this information may be generated by the association itself; some may come from the churches or their organizations. State and Southern Baptist Convention agencies generate large amounts of information which often is communicated through the association to the Baptist constituency. These same groups often need information from or about the churches and they turn to the association as their best source.

B. *Types of communication networks.* In every organizational system, such as the Baptist denomination, there are three types of communication networks: (1) formal, (2) subformal or informal, and (3) personal. Formal communications are official statements and reports such as a treasurer's report, or the clerk's minutes of associational meetings, or where financial assistance is given, director of missions' monthly report to the state Baptist office and the Home Mission Board.

Informal communication networks grow up in every organization. Sometimes these messages may be transmitted over the formal network channels, even though the message may be both generated and communicated informally. For example, the director of missions' formal report may never mention a problem in a particular church. The informal communication of information about a particular problem may be the most important item of information exchanged between the associational and the state missions director.

Leaders in the association may transmit some information acting as persons rather than in their capacity as office holders. Such news tends to travel faster than formal communications since individuals often do not take time to verify sources and assure accuracy.

C. *Communication instruments.* Internal communications in the association travel over a variety of channels. Direct mail, telephone calls, and printed newsletters are most widely used. Much communication is by word of mouth, whether by announcements from the pulpits, or informal comments at the post office or bowling alley.

Many associations are now using the mass media of newspapers, radio, and television to transmit to external target groups and, on occasion, to their own constituency.

Monthly newsletters can convey much specific information to church leaders and others the association seeks to serve. Someone has said that "People are usually down on what they're not up on."

If people are to become involved in associational programs they must be informed about what is available, the group the program serves, when and where the activity is being conducted. Events of widespread interest involving large numbers of people may best be publicized through newsletters mailed out to all church leaders. Direct mail and telephone reminders are better for reaching small groups such as committees of the association.

Usually the director of missions is expected to be responsible for the publicity and public relations programs of the association. He will be wise to enlist qualified experts in the area who can assist in this important and highly skilled work. Working arrangements may be worked out with one or more churches for the shared purchase and use of printing, folding and addressing equipment when the use of commercial facilities is not feasible.

The director of missions should cultivate friendships with editors of newspapers serving his area and news directors of radio and television stations in the area. He should master the art of writing good news stories and submit them to the media when the stories are still news.

D. *Associational records and reports.* An important aspect of the associational communication system is the preparation, processing, and distribution of records and reports.

For example, the committee on the annual session (sometimes called the committee on order of business or the time, place, and preacher committee) plans an interesting and helpful program for the annual associational meeting. This report, with as much useful information as is readily available about speakers, choirs, and other groups to be on the program, should be conveyed to the associational office and follow-up processing done. Facilities at the scheduled place of meeting must be checked to assure they are adequate for the activities planned. Then, on a carefully timed schedule, information is distributed to associational officers, to the various program leaders in the churches, with interesting news stories with a personal interest angle being distributed to news media (newspapers, radio, and television) serving the area.

In processing committee reports the associational office should send duplicate copies of committee minutes to all committee members and keep on file in the association office a complete file of minutes on all committees, boards, councils, et cetera, of the association.

When the association does not maintain an associational office with a secretary, either paid or volunteer, responsibility for the records system rests upon the associational clerk. Records, committee reports, financial records, and minutes should be maintained for a specified length of time. A permanent file of the printed annual minutes and the uniform church letters, submitted annually from the churches, should be maintained as a basic source of continuing information about the association. Dated copies of the constitution and bylaws and any copies of histories of the association or any of its affiliated churches should be kept.

Records such as property deeds, charters of incorporation, and inventories of associational property should be kept in a safe-deposit box to prevent possible loss by fire, theft, or vandalism.

4. Securing and Administering Financial Resources and Facilities

After the association has considered the needs it will seek to meet, set its objectives and goals, established the requisite organization, and planned for the staff of both paid and volunteer leaders needed to operate the desired programs, it must then consider the matters of making an equitable, comprehensive budget, set about procuring the needed financial resources, and establish a budget control and accounting system that will guarantee the proper handling of all funds and other resources.

A. *The work of the finance committee in preparing the budget.* The finance committee of the association has the responsibility of planning a budget that will seek to allocate available resources to these programs considered by the association to have the highest priority. The committee should have full access to any survey of community needs, self-study reports, and decisions and recommendations growing out of the use of the *Annual Associational Planning Guide* or the *Associational Strategy Planning Guide.*

Wherever possible the finance committee will seek to find ways of including support for those programs selected by the planning groups as having the highest priority in the distribution of available financial resources. Associational program leaders, the paid staff responsible for administering any associational programs, and any other interested Baptist leader should have opportunity to appear before the finance committee to discuss the financial needs of existing or proposed programs.

After receiving information about the anticipated costs of programs and personnel, the finance committee will need to survey possible sources. Most funds normally come from the churches who designate either a percentage of their total budget (usually from 2 percent to 5 percent) or specify a fixed amount to be provided from the church for the work of the association.

When churches are fully informed about the programs they are seeking to accomplish through the association, when all churches participate in the budget-making process, more generous and dependable support may be expected from the churches. The finance committee should present the proposed budget to the executive board for approval and then to the association for adoption.

Other sources may include shared support for certain mission projects and support of the director of missions by the Baptist state convention, the Home Mission Board, and, on rare occasions, other denominational agencies. Some associational programs may be partly or fully self-supporting, such as a day-care center, a seminary extension center, a home for the elderly, or an associational camp.

State stewardship leaders and the Southern Baptist Stewardship Commission staff are available for counsel in helping to plan, promote, and conduct a stewardship education program and budget campaign. "Stewardship Decision Night," bringing together, two or three months before budget subscription time, the pastors and key decision makers from the churches in the association, has been very effective in presenting the challenge and opportunity of associational, state and world missions. Make use also of the *Stewardship Development Guide for Baptist Associations* and material produced by the Stewardship Commission, SBC.

B. *Administering associational funds.* Support for the association is enhanced when associational officials follow sound practices of financial management. All persons handling money received by the association should be bonded. Funds received should be counted, recorded, and deposited promptly in the bank. These steps may be taken by a paid employee in the associational office or by the associational treasurer.

The association should send to each church treasurer each year a supply of remittance slips and envelopes pre-addressed to the associational office, which the church treasurers may use monthly in sending in gifts from the churches. The monthly report of the associational treasurer should indicate receipts of all kinds from each church and other sources, if any.

All disbursements should be by check on authorization by the budget or by the person designated as purchasing officer for the association. This could be the director of missions or some other paid staff member. No purchases should be made or paid for without a purchase order bearing the signature of the purchasing agent. A record should be kept of all purchases and all disbursements.

When the association has unordained paid employees, the federal government requires the securing of an "employers identification number" by filing form SS4. Each nonexempt employee should sign an

Principles of Administration

"Employee Withholding Exemption Certificate" (Form W-4), which should be kept on file with the association's financial records. Income taxes should be withheld from all unordained employees with quarterly remittances to the Internal Revenue Service using Form 941, "Employee's Quarterly Tax Return." Social Security payments should be made on behalf of all unordained employees. Ordained employees make their Social Security payments when filing their income tax returns.

Reports of the record of contributions should be made regularly to each church, to the executive board, and annually to the association. An annual audit of all financial records should be conducted by competent personnel not connected with administering of those funds.

C. *Securing and maintaining adequate facilities.* As the work of the association develops in scope, it will need facilities to accomplish its work. By facilities we mean all kinds of property, buildings, equipment, and supplies that are useful in enabling the association to accomplish more effectively the work it is undertaking to do.

What facilities are needed? The basic principle is that "form follows function." An association with no paid staff will require very little in the way of facilities. The associational clerk and moderator may be able to keep in their homes or offices all the associational records, files, and equipment.

When associations add paid staff members and institutionalized programs, facilities will be needed to accomplish desired objectives. An adequate administrative program will provide for the securing, maintaining, inventorying, and protecting of the association's facilities.

When should facilities be added? The employment of a director of missions will usually be accompanied by the provision through rental or purchase or housing allowance of a home for the director. A suitable office and equipment essential for effective office operation will also be needed. Financial resources of the association and the level of interest in supporting associational work will be major factors in determining the facilities provided for associational staff and programs.

Associations with limited financial resources immediately available may provide a housing allowance for the director of missions adequate to provide both a home and an office. Office space for the association will often be made available by one of the affiliated churches. It may be rented in some public building. As resources become available and the need is apparent, the association may build or purchase its own headquarters building. E. C. Watson has specified the normal requirements for an associational office.[3]

The offices of the association may be located in a multipurpose building, housing several programs of the association. The Tulsa Baptist Center provides quarters for the director of missions and his staff, for the Baptist student program serving an adjacent university campus, for seminary extension courses, and for committee meetings and conferences related to Baptist work in the area. They also provide offices for the occasional use of the state Baptist Foundation representatives and for other denominational leaders visiting the association.

In Louisville, Kentucky, the Long Run Baptist Association built a multipurpose Baptist center providing offices for the association, facilities for a day-care center, a student center for the adjacent medical sciences center. The building also provides facilities for weekday ministries to the neighboring community and also facilities for the East Baptist Church. Their building is in almost constant use around the clock, seven days a week. Many associations own mission centers. Some own and operate homes for the elderly, nursing homes, and hospitals. Several own and operate camps. Many associations purchase sites for new churches, holding title to such property until a sponsoring church can be enlisted or until a new mission congregation can assume responsibility of ownership. Associations should consider with care the financial burden of the ownership and operation of programs that may prove to be a financial drain on other important activities of the association. Frequently, facilities used only occasionally in associational programs can better be rented or leased from others. Camp facilities are an example. E. C. Watson observes: Camps are expensive, and only those associations with rather liberal financial support can afford them. Many associations should consider seriously the possibility of using state convention and Southen Baptist Convention facilities or renting camping facilities before embarking upon a project to provide its own. Also, the relative value of the camp in comparison with other needs should be considered.[4]

If the association provides a home for the director of missions rather than a housing allowance, the location of the home should be determined by convenience of access, particularly if it will also be used as an office center for the association. In selecting a location for a separate office, consideration should be given to adequate parking for associational leaders attending meetings, the accessibility of the office to the whole association, and the possibility of locating the office in a multipurpose building along with other associational programs.

The associational office is an information and administrative center for the entire association and will need adequate equipment and supplies if it is to perform its designed purpose. Such equipment should include a typewriter, duplicating equipment, file cabinets, a drawing board for design and layout work, dictation equipment, a calculator, bulletin board, tract rack, motion picture and slide and filmstrip projectors, and screens, tape recorders, cameras, and adequate storage for such equipment and office supplies and literature available for distribution. Heating and cooling equipment, if not integral to the building, should be provided.

As the association launches other programs such as weekday centers and mission centers, the plans should provide for adequate buildings and equipment.

An annual inventory should be made of all associational property, including invested funds, buildings and equipment, and supplies. A permanent record should be kept of these items along with a record of maintenance and repairs. The associational properties committee should be responsible for such an inventory and for the inspection and maintenance of associational property. Responsibility for the supervision of the maintenance of the associational building should be assigned to a staff member of the association who will maintain consultation with the properties committee in supervising the custodial and maintenance personnel.

The associational properties committee should receive requests from the program and service leaders of the association, evaluate the requests, and communicate their recommendations to the finance committee in advance of the time for the preparation of the associational budget. After the budget has become effective, purchases of equipment and other facilities can be made according to the purchasing policy of the association.

5. Evaluation and Feedback

An ongoing administrative function no association should neglect is that of evaluation in terms of objectives.

This step in the administrative process is often referred to as "control." It involves the appraisal of results to determine how well other administrative functions are being carried out. It measures performance of all associational organizations and leaders and can be useful in motivating individuals to contribute their best efforts. Evaluation makes possible the recognition of achievement. It is essential for further planning and programming.

A. *Evaluate on the basis of objectives.* Evaluation assumes some standard of measurement. Associational work should be evaluated in terms of effectiveness in achieving associational objectives. Associational leaders should ask: Are objectives clear? How well are they being achieved? What are the reasons for specific successes or failures? How may effectiveness be increased? What does "feedback" from various constituencies indicate to be needed, such as changes in structure, programs, personnel, facilities? Are associational activities, personnel, and budgets reflective of basic objectives consciously determined by the association?

B. *Who is responsible for evaluation?* Since evaluation and feedback should bring improvement in functioning, self-evaluation by associational leaders will be more conducive to improvement.

Within the organization structure of the association the associational council should perform continuing evaluation and feedback. This group includes program leaders able to initiate prompt changes in associational activities that are not contributing to achieving objectives.

A special long-range planning committee or steering committee using the *Associational Strategy Planning Guide* may perform some very important evaluation and feedback.

Either of these groups should bring reports to the executive board and ultimately to the association to incorporate needed changes into the structure and programs of the association.

In some associations it may be advisable to secure a competent consultant from outside the association to evaluate its structure and functioning. Sometimes groups inside the association find it harder to maintain objectivity and independence of judgment because of their identification with one or more programs of the association. Insiders may be the targets of informal social pressure from colleagues who want their activities endorsed.

C. *When should evaluation and feedback occur?* Every meeting of the associational council should provide some time for evaluation. As plans are made for any associational activities, the question should be raised as to how that activity may make the maximum contribution to associational objectives and meet the needs of the churches.

The council may schedule an annual retreat for evaluation and annual planning. Such a meeting should include on its agenda a careful evaluation of all associational programs, with decisions regarding needed changes and additions.

D. *What should be evaluated?*

1. The director of missions and other staff members may begin the process by making a self-evaluation of themselves and their work over the past year, noting strengths and weaknesses, stating personal and professional objectives, and goals for the coming year. This might become the basis for discussing with the associational council changes in

emphases, schedules, job descriptions, or even changes in personnel.

2. The organizational structure of the association should be evaluated. Does it enhance or hinder the effectiveness of the association? Is there more organization than is being used effectively? Would another organizational structure be more useful? How well are leaders in organizations and committees functioning?

3. Associational programs should be evaluated. Have some outlived their usefulness? Do some need to be added? Are they meeting real needs for the churches? Who is being served? Who attends meetings? Are some churches making no use of associational programs? Why?

E. *Corrective actions should follow evaluation.* Diagnosing associational problems is largely wasted effort if no course corrections are made. The moderator and director of missions should assure that indicated changes are incorporated in future associational work.

NOTES

1. Ray Johns, *Executive Responsibility* (New York: Association Press, 1966), p. 178f.

2. *Ibid.*, pp. 90–92.

3. E. C. Watson, *Superintendent of Missions for an Association* (Atlanta: Home Mission Board, 1969), pp. 96–101.

4. E. C. Watson, *Associational Base Design* (Atlanta: Home Mission Board, 1972), p. 244.

7.

Director of Missions

The work of the association is so crucial to the effective functioning of the churches and as a vital link in the communications and assistance channel of the denomination, that more and more associations have turned to a divinely called and equipped worker to give full-time direction to the work of the association. About three-fourths of the 1,192 Baptist associations now have a paid administrator giving leadership in associational activities.

The prevailing title used now by most associations is that of director of missions. A title widely used earlier and still used in some associations is that of associational missionary. Some associations choose to use other titles for their chief administrator.

1. Role Expectations

The churches, their leaders and their members, have certain expectations of the director of missions. Past experience will have affected concepts that the people have of the office. To some the director of missions will be seen as a convenient supply minister, available to conduct worship services in the absence of a pastor. Others may see him primarily as a religious educator giving aggressive leadership to the programs of Bible teaching, membership and leadership training, missionary education, et cetera, within the churches and in general associational meetings of various kinds. Expectations of others focus upon his missionary activities with responsibilities for establishing new mission ministries and providing services for neglected and troubled groups within the community. Some see him as camp director; others as conference leader. Pastors and churches confronting difficulties may see him primarily as shepherd and counselor, as reconciler and peacemaker.

Leaders in the state Baptist convention and among the agencies of the Southern Baptist Convention will often see him as the "key man" in interpreting and promoting programs in which they have a special interest.

In the community, expectations may focus upon leadership in civic and moral crusades against threatened or entrenched evils affecting the entire community. The indigents and the transients may discover him to be a source of emergency help. Individuals and families facing special problems may find him a sympathetic and well-informed referral agent who can direct them to the best possible sources of assistance.

To a secretary in his office and to other staff members under his supervision there will be expectations of fair and competent administration, Christian colleagueship, and leadership that maintains a clear view of objectives and an enthusiasm for the ministry of the association.

What has been said here about the director of missions will apply to other members of the associational professional staff in those associations with such employees.

2. Qualifications

Obviously, a person in such a significant role of Christian leadership should himself be a person with genuine Christian experience that is healthy, growing, and easily shared. Joy, satisfaction, and effectiveness in associational work are enhanced when one has not only a clear sense of call to the ministry but also a commitment to a particular task of associational leadership.

A call to serve is a call to get ready. The director of missions and other staff members should have sufficient formal training to give them competence in the work they are expected to do and to maintain the respect of the people with whom they work. Experience in both church and associational work is extremely beneficial.

In a time when organizations of all kinds, and particularly denominational organizations have been under attack, the director of missions and other staff members should be aware of the necessity and values of organizational structure and activity and be committed to enabling the association to achieve its designed objectives. Associational director of missions should be committed to the Baptist denomination and be continually seeking to improve their functioning. The director of missions should be prepared to master the skills involved in effective administration, continually seeking to improve his ability in performing the administrative functions discussed extensively in the preceding chapter.

3. Procedure for Election

Each association is, of course, free to determine its own procedures for the seeking and electing of a director of missions. When financial support of the director of missions is shared by the state convention and the Home Mission Board, their policies and procedures should be studied carefully. The responsibility for bringing a recommendation may be assigned to the associational personnel committee or to some other standing committee or special committee chosen for this purpose. The associational constitution should state clearly who has this responsibility and how the process is to be initiated. Upon the authorization of the association or its executive board the committee could begin its work, keeping in mind the guidelines set by the state convention and Home Mission Board when joint support is anticipated. Motivation for more extensive participation and support of associational work is enhanced by placing major responsibility for selecting of the director of missions with the association rather than the state convention.

The personnel committee or some other designated committee could well begin by a prayerful consideration of the objectives of the association and the contribution that the new director of missions is expected to make toward the achieving of these objectives. The job description for the director of missions should be studied and revised as needed in light of current circumstances. The particular qualifications needed to meet the special needs of the association should be discussed. After this important preliminary work has been done, the committee may begin to assemble the names of prospective directors of missions and gather from appropriate sources information about their competence as associational administrators.

Information should be secured from churches where the individual has served in the past, from the colleges and seminaries that he attended, from businessmen able to evaluate his business integrity and management skills. Denominational leaders who know of his interest in and commitment to the denomination should be consulted by the committee. After discussing one or more possibilities in the light of all of this information, the committee may arrange for an interview where the work of the association may be discussed more fully with the potential director of missions. He should be given the opportunity to visit the association at its expense for an extensive evaluation of the possibilities of service, for conferences with the associational leaders and a careful analysis of the community served by the association.

E. C. Watson [1] lists thirteen items that should be discussed with the prospective director of missions. The committee should have definite information regarding associational policies with respect to each of the items mentioned. These items include salary, travel expenses, living quarters, retirement benefits, allowances, vacations, off-duty days, policies with respect to revivals and pulpit supplies, moving expenses, job description, and procedures for terminating services.

When staff members other than the director of missions are being employed, opportunities should be given for extensive conferences between the prospective employee and the director of missions and other paid staff members as well as the personnel committee and other leaders of the association. Initiative in the selection and recommendation of secretaries, assistants and other staff members should be given to the person to whom the new staff member will report. The personnel committee should be involved in interviews and in making the final recommendation to employ.

4. Salary and Benefits

In his instructions to the seventy, Jesus underscored a basic principle regarding the financial support of the ministry. "The laborer deserves his wages" (Luke 10:7, RSV).

With the steadily rising cost of living, it is appropriate for the association, employing a director of missions, to secure sufficient financial resources to provide a salary commensurate with the living standard of the area and in keeping with his ability, preparation and experience.

A housing allowance should be provided that is adequate to secure a comfortable home if the association does not own and provide a home for the director of missions. The director of missions will be expected to travel extensively throughout the association and a plan for travel expense reimbursement should be adopted. Fifteen or more cents per mile for travel related to associational business would be appropriate. Most associations will provide for expenses incurred by the director of missions in attending the state Baptist convention and Southern Baptist Convention and certain other denominational meetings designated by the associational executive board.

Provisions for participation in continuing education programs, such as those conducted by some of the Baptist seminaries, will usually pay rich dividends in improved performance and high morale.

The association should participate in the Southern Baptist Annuity Board retirement program on behalf of its employees whenever coverage is not supplied by the state convention and the Home Mission Board (for jointly employed staff). Medical coverage, travel insurance, and related protection aids both the director of missions and the association in the sense of security and peace of mind with such provisions.

All salary, benefits,and home or house allowance arrangements should be clearly stated in writing to avoid subsequent misunderstanding.

Included in such a written statement should be the approved arrangements for days off each week, vacation time, sick leave, holidays, the number of days per year the director of missions may be involved in engagements outside the association, and an understanding regarding remuneration received by the director of missions for services to churches within the association.

The salary of the director of missions should be reviewed each year and adjustments made in light of changes in the cost of living and the association's desire to express appreciation for effective work.

As a service to itself as well as to the director of missions the association should provide adequate office space and equipment and a full-time or part-time secretary. If the association feels it cannot afford paid secretarial service, arrangements should be made for dependable volunteer workers to perform this service so the time of the director of missions may be given to administrative and ministerial duties.

A job description for the director of missions should be prepared by the executive board or its personnel committee in consultation with the director of missions. Similar job descriptions should be developed for all other paid employees of the association.

When a new director of missions is being employed, the representatives of the association should give a clear and accurate picture of the circumstances of the association, its problems as well as its possibilities. The job description should be discussed together and any changes mutually agreed upon should be approved officially by the executive board.

5. Developing Leadership Skills

A. *Types of leaders.* One may observe four basic types of leaders in church and denominational work. The autocratic leader insists on making most of the decisions personally. He considers his way to be the only right way. He has a compulsion to dominate any group of which he is a part. Groups led by autocratic leaders develop very little leadership abilities within the group. They are content to leave the decisions to the leader or else become antagonistic and drop out.

A paternalistic leader is likely to boast of "taking care" of his people. He does favors for them and expects them, in return, to do his bidding.

The laissez-faire leader lets everything muddle along. He practically abdicates any leadership responsibility.

The kind of leadership usually appropriate in church and denominational life is a democratic leadership. The democratic leader sees himself as an equipper and enabler who helps people to grow, to assume responsibility, and to develop leadership skills. The democratic leader helps the group to move toward the achievement of goals which they have helped to set. He studies carefully each member of the group and seeks to encourage each individual to become involved in what he can best contribute to group activities and goals. A democratic leader is open to new ideas both from members of the group and from outside sources. He is willing to accept decisions made by the group.

Paul seemed to be thinking of the equipping, enabling leader in Ephesians 4:11–13. The leaders, whether apostles, prophets, evangelists, pastors, or teachers, were given to the church "To prepare all of God's people for the work of Christian service, to build up the body of Christ. And so we shall all come together to oneness in our faith and in our knowledge of the Son of God; we shall become mature men, reaching to the very height of Christ's full stature" (Eph. 4:12–13, TEV):

B. *Leading others to spiritual maturity.* In associational work and in the work of the church, God's purpose is that each individual should grow spiritually in order to reach his full potential and perform the ministry that God has equipped and called him to perform. The democratic leader will help interpret, support, and carry out the work that the association has planned and begun.

In bureaucratic administrative arrangements in business and industry the scalar principle of exercising authority from the top down is the prevalent pattern. In such an organization it is assumed that the needs of the organization take precedence over the needs of individuals. The individual is expected to subordinate his own goals and needs for the good of the organization. But in church and denominational administration the integrity, welfare, and needs of the individual become as important as the welfare of an organization. The effective leader in associational work will be sensitive to the needs of each individual participant in associational organizations and activities and will develop plans and programs that, as frequently as possible, achieve both individual as well as associational goals and needs.

J. C. Bradley describes this kind of Christian leadership as "transactional administration." "Autocratic direction and control fails to call forth the kind of commitment which would make available the full resources of those affected. The cost of lowered commitment, lowered motivation, and lowered self-direction would far offset any gains obtained by unilateral decisions for the 'good of the organization.' " [2]

6. The Relationships of the Director of Missions

A. *Priority of the association.* As with the pastor in the church the director of missions is the "key man" in the work of the association. He is so regarded by leaders in the affiliated churches and by denominational leaders in other associations, the state Baptist convention and the SBC agencies.

The first responsibility of the director of missions is to the association where he serves. In almost all cases this principle is now operative in Baptist associations even when the director of missions is supported in whole or in part by other denominational agencies. The exact degree of supervision and decision making in the selection process varies from one state convention to another.

In some states considerable control is maintained by the state convention. In the Southern Baptist Convention of California the Cooperative Missions Division, in its statement of *Policies and Procedures*, states: The selection of the missionary (director of missions) will be initiated by the association or the Missions Committee (of the association) in conference with the Director of Cooperative Missions (of the state convention). The association will nominate for election by the Executive Board (of the state convention) upon the approval of the Personnel Department of the Home Mission Board. No person shall be employed except by full agreement of the association, Executive Board, and the Home Mission Board through the Personnel Department.

Baptist in Indiana have followed a plan by which control of the selection of the director of missions was gradually passed to the association as it developed in its support of the director of missions. If the association provided less than one-fourth of the support, the director of missions was selected and placed on the field by the state convention. If the association provided as much as one-fourth of the support, the convention chose the director of missions subject to the approval of the association. If the association provided as much as one-half of the support, the association chose the director of missions subject to the approval of the state convention. If the association provided more than three-fourths of the support, it chose the director of missions.

On the other hand, some associations have sufficient resources to employ and support their director of missions without requesting shared support by the state convention or the Home Mission Board. Such associations have full responsibility for determining qualifications and procedures for employment. Sometimes these associations will have other employees jointly supported by the state convention and the Home Mission Board, even though the director of missions is not jointly employed and supported. These variations indicate the ability of autonomous Baptist groups to work out harmonious and generally effective working relationships, enabling them to respond individually or cooperatively to urgent spiritual needs in the area.

B. *Supervision of the director of missions.* Within the association the director of missions is responsible to the association, working under the supervision of the executive board and its executive or administrative committee. In some associations this supervisory group is the personnel committee.

C. *Supervision by the director of missions.* The director of missions will supervise secretarial personnel and any other employees of the association. In larger associations he may supervise a group of professional employees to whom supervisory responsibility may be delegated.

In all his supervisory relationships the director of missions should look upon associational employees as Christian colleagues, each with assigned tasks. An atmosphere of mutual trust and support for fellow staff members should prevail. Each member of the team should be expected to know his or her assigned tasks and perform those tasks at the right time and in the right manner.[3]

D. *Relation to pastors, church staff·members, and leaders.* The director of missions should cherish and cultivate good relationships with the pastors and church staff members in the association. His goal should be to help each to succeed in being and doing all that God has purposed for them. In his relationships with pastors, staff members, and all associational leaders the director of missions' relationships should be characterized by open communications, mutual trust, and mutual support. In all relationships he will practice those procedures that enhance Christian maturity, achieve Christian fellowship, and accomplish Christian mission.

E. *Relationships to other denominational leaders.* In many cases the director of missions will have a reporting relationship and receive, in some cases, some supervision by the state missions director. Those receiving joint support are responsible for monthly reports on their activities to the state convention and the Home Mission Board.

In addition to these formal relationships the superintendent and other associational leaders are cooperatively related to other associations, to the state Baptist convention, its departments and agencies, and to the several agencies of the Southern Baptist Convention. As noted earlier in discussing the "systems concept" of church and denominational organization, the association, though autonomous, is a willing part of this remarkable system of denominational relationships. Each component in this system has its own subsystems, and each in turn, is a part of a larger "supersystem," all of which may have interdependent relationships with each other.

Director of Missions

For example, the Sunday School Department of the Sunday School Board may relate to an associational missions director and its Sunday School director in planning an associational clinic on outreach through church buses. The Seminary Extension Department, jointly supported by the six Southern Baptist Convention seminaries, may relate to the associational director of missions in establishing and conducting a seminary extension center. The associational director of Church Training may be related to the Church Training leaders in one or more churches as he provides leadership training or consultation to "subsystem" leaders in the church program organizations of the churches. All are bound up in an interdependent network of relationships.

F. *Relations to community groups.* The director of missions represents the association in relating to various community, public school, business, political, social and welfare organizations, and to other religious groups functioning in the area served by the association. In some cases the association will work cooperatively with these groups in pursuit of common goals affecting the people in the area.

There may be cooperation with schools or civic groups on such matters as alcohol, education, or drug abuse. There may be cooperation with an interdenominational ministers conference in establishing or improving chaplaincy services in public hospitals, penal institutions, or other special groups. The director of missions may initiate or maintain cooperative relationships with the department of public welfare and other religious groups in a procedure for validating requests from indigents and transients for assistance, and for providing such assistance when appropriate.

In the Gaston Association in North Carolina the director of missions is contacted by the welfare department when valid requests come for help that cannot be supplied through regular department channels. The association is organized to respond to such requests, ministering in a spirit of Christian love.

G. *Basis for relationships.* The association is by its very nature and history an organization providing meaningful relationships to participants in its programs. The New Testament describes churches exercising responsible concern for one another. Early Baptist associations manifested this mutual concern, support, and assistance provided by the association to affiliated churches.

These Christian relationships are free and voluntary, subject to the authoritative precept and example of the Lord Jesus Christ. Wherever concern and responsibility are shared, the association through its staff may enter into relationships with other Baptist agencies and groups and with community organizations concerned for meeting needs of concern to the association.

7. Performing Leadership Tasks

The ultimate evidence of effectiveness on the part of the director of missions is his ability to lead the association in performing her tasks.

A. One of his major responsibilities is that of leading the association to be a Baptist interchurch fellowship where there is open communication, mutual trust, and mutual support.

B. The director of missions will frequently need to provide pastoral care and counsel for the pastors, church staff members, and their families.

C. He will administer the mission work the churches do cooperatively through the association. This may include the work of establishing and assisting new churches, new missions, and conducting mission ministries of various kinds. Some mission ministries may be ongoing year around, including activities such as operating a day-care program, providing services for hospitals, jails, nursing homes, and other institutions. Some ministries such as services to migrant laborers may be seasonal.

Some associations conduct cooperatively a radio and/or television ministry. Some have a ministry to students attending local colleges, professional or trade schools. Many associations operate seminary extension centers providing needed training for both ministers and laymen.

The above responsibilities of the association and its director of missions may be grouped together under the heading of "Cooperative Activities Program." The *Annual Associational Planning Guide* lists seven such programs, recognizing that not many associations should have all of these seven, while some associations might need to add others not mentioned. The seven suggested "Cooperative Activities Programs" are: (1) Cooperative Missions; (2) Youth Ministries; (3) Student Ministries; (4) Community Penetration; (5) Mass Media Communication (newspapers, radio, television); (6) Continuing Ministerial Education; (7) Ministerial Fellowship.

D. Another major responsibility of the director of missions is directing the program of church development. This involves providing and interpreting information for the churches, providing training for church leaders, and providing resources to church leaders in their work, whether in Sunday School, Church Training, Woman's Missionary Union, Brotherhood, church music, church library, or church recreation.

The *Annual Associational Planning Guide* [4] suggests the grouping of these "Church Assistance Programs" in three categories:

> (1) Church Emphasis Programs
>   a. Evangelism Development
>   b. Stewardship Development
>   c. Vocational Guidance
>   d. Family Services
> (2) Church Organization Programs
>   a. Sunday School Development
>   b. Church Training Development
>   c. Church Music Development
>   d. Brotherhood Development
>   e. Woman's Missionary Union Development
> (3) Church Services Programs
>   a. Church Administration Development
>   b. Church Library Development
>   c. Church Recreation Development

8. The Director of Missions as Agent of Change

Jesus came to this world in order to bring about change. He challenged the established patterns of life calling for changed attitudes and

Principles of Administration

behavior, saying "You have heard that it was said . . . . But I say to you . . ." (Matt. 5:21–22, 27–28, 33–34, 38–39, 43–44, RSV).

In calling the disciples Simon and Andrew, Jesus said, "Follow me and I will make you become . . ." (Mark 1:17, RSV). But most people prefer to remain as they are. They resist change even when it clearly is a part of God's design. Churches and associations also tend to resist change.

In his book, *The Change Agent*, Lyle E. Schaller tells of the Hale's Corners Church "founded in 1841 at the crossroads community which included a blacksmith shop, a post office in the general store, and a tavern which served as an overnight stop on the stagecoach runs. In 1900 the congregation included 113 members. By 1955 this figure had increased to 117, of whom 103 lived on farms. In 1964, with the opening of the new highway a mile away, Hale's Corners was beginning to look more like a suburban community and the membership of the church had more than doubled to 243." [5] In 1965 the congregation completed a new church building, but by 1971, though the population in the community had doubled the 1965 figure, church membership stood at 219.

Pastors had become so frustrated by the unwillingness of the congregation to change to adjust its program to the rapidly changing needs of the community that two pastors had left the ministry for other careers and a third was contemplating similar action. The church seemingly could not escape from its preoccupation with maintenance and survival goals to move on to mission goals for the church. Schaller concluded that the Hale's Corners Church, "despite an influx of new members, a new building program, and a succession of future-oriented ministers, the congregation continues to act on the assumption that this is a small rural church where institutional survival is the most important factor to be considered in making policy decisions." [6]

It is the responsibility of the director of missions to assist churches like the one at Hale's Corners to make the changes in attitude and priorities that will enable them to respond to the rapidly changing needs around them. To become an effective "change agent" the director of missions will need to understand what leads both individuals and organizations to

126

change.

A church or an association tends to respond to the pressures and demands made upon it in terms of its own sense of mission. Its own understanding of who it is and what it exists to do determines its priorities, its allocation of finances, facilities, and personnel. An association that has majored in the past on fellowship, evangelism, and leadership training may, because of the pressing needs in its community, establish and operate a day-care center, housing for the elderly, a ministry to migrant laborers, or other institutionalized ministries. People act in keeping with their value systems, out of their priorities.

Bringing about change in organizations involves three stages— unfreezing, changing, and refreezing. The director of missions can help bring about needed changes by creating conditions that cause church or associational leaders to question their old habits, assumptions, and attitudes. He helps leaders and other participants to identify alternative ways of doing things before deciding what should be done and how.

The process of changing is not simple or easy. People often become confused and uncomfortable when they abandon the security of old habits and assumptions. Nevertheless, to deal with frozen patterns of behavior, the group must pass through the uncomfortable stage of unfreezing. Through the process of evaluation and feedback the association or church can discover if the newly adopted programs or procedures are effective, measured by the extent to which they enable the organization to reach its objectives. If the feedback is negative—indicating that the new patterns are not effective, then further exploration and experimentation with other alternatives must precede refreezing at another, more effective level of performance.

To be an effective change agent the director of missions must know the history of the association and its churches, their successes and their failures. Elaine Dickson has stated: Past successes tend to generate the belief that what produced success in the past will continue to produce success regardless of the new forces which have been introduced into the situation. On the other hand, past failures lead people to conclude that whatever has failed once can never succeed again. Most organizations have a catalog, though unwritten, of some things which can be expected to succeed and other things which cannot be expected to succeed. Only in understanding these historical dimensions of a church's (or association's) experience can the change agent understand the conditions under which the system will be able to break free from its past to commit itself to something new.[7]

Forces for change are present in any association. The director of missions should lead the association to make a wise choice of change targets. "This requires astute assessment of the changeability of a system at any particular point in time." [8] Dickson comments further that "successful change is most easily achieved by widespread participation of the persons being affected by change." [9]

Enduring change takes time. A church or an association may make temporary and superficial changes to respond to and comply with the demands of autocratic leaders. But if change is to endure, the value systems of the people involved in the association must be transformed and new norms of appropriate actions be developed. These processes take time. Directors of missions or pastors who move frequently from one situation to another will not likely be instrumental in bringing about significant deep level changes.

Some directors of missions will need help in becoming change agents. Some may prefer to be protectors of the status quo rather than agents of change. Those who do see the needs for change and who wish to encourage and facilitate it can develop skills in functioning effectively as an agent of change.

9. Continuing Education for Directors of Missions

The preparation of the director of missions for the effective performance of his tasks is—or should be—a continuing process. "When you're through learning you're through!" applies to the director of missions as it does to most other leadership positions.

A. *Forms of continuing education.* An adequate program for continuing education for directors of missions must take into account the fact that we are dealing with mature adults capable of self-direction with intrinsic motivation. Directors of missions bring to any continuing educational learning experiences their own rich experience which they can share with others and which becomes a base upon which to build new insights and skills. Learning experiences should be planned less around the transmission of information and more upon the sharing of experiences and the analysis of that experience. To insist upon a director of missions returning to the typical school setting to receive information from some expert is, in a sense, a way of rejecting the director of missions own experience. Whenever an adult's experience is devalued or ignored, he is likely to perceive this as not only rejecting his experience but rejecting him as a person. The continuing education program, therefore, should convey respect for adult learners by making use of their experience as a resource for learning for themselves and others.

Continuing education for directors of missions should be responsive to the particular needs and demands of such a role. Although the director of missions tasks may be similar in many respects to his previous responsibilities as a pastor, church staff member, et cetera, there are peculiar responsibilities resting upon him that demand specialized training.

Continuing education for directors of missions should focus upon specific areas of responsibility rather than be organized around classical theological disciplines. It will be more readily accepted if it is problem-centered rather than subject-centered. A curriculum could be organized around problem areas, perhaps with a different but sequential set of problems each year, and with the sequence of learning within each unit moving from field experience to theory and principles, and from foundational knowledge to skilled practice to field application.

As long as the life span of an individual was longer than the time necessary for major cultural change, then education as the transmission of culture was valid and the role of the teacher as a transmitter was valid. But now the life span of an individual, up to seventy-two years, is considerably longer than the time in which major cultural changes are

Principles of Administration

occurring in contemporary society. This is particularly true in the rapidly changing events confronted by the director of missions. New problems are emerging in community life, in denominational programming, and in the practice of ministry. This makes all the more urgent a continuing education program for directors of missions that helps them to become more effective leaders in planned change. Such a continuing education program should shift its major focus from the transmission of content to developing an understanding of process and providing the tools for inquiry, analysis and planned change.

The director of missions will be dealing with ministers whose actual experience in ministry may be quite different from what they had been led to expect in their years of formal preparation. They need help in learning who they are and how they can respond to the challenging expectations for them as ministers. The continuing education program for the director of missions should equip him to assist the ministers with whom he works to discover, develop and celebrate each minister's gifts and prepare them to serve as catalysts and implementers of change institutionally, ethically, theologically, and personally. If directors of missions are to equip ministers in the association and themselves to become effective change agents, they will need to develop their skills and help ministers to develop skills in building high trust levels between the minister and his congregation, between the director of missions and his constituency.

Continuing education should help participants develop interpersonal competence and sensitivity. It should provide insight and skill in organization development and in long-range planning.

Continuing education for directors of missions may involve no academic credit, but it can involve various degree programs in colleges and seminaries. Director of missions who have completed their basic seminary degree would do well to consider the Doctor of Ministry programs now available in Southern Baptist seminaries.

B. *Scheduling continuing education opportunities.* A comprehensive program of continuing education for directors of missions should

Director of Missions

utilize training opportunities on the job. This could take advantage of the home study units now being provided by the Seminary Extension Department and similar programs from other sources. It could involve the supervised field experience programs of the Doctor of Ministry degree programs in Baptist seminaries.

Some such work can be held very profitably on the campuses of the seminaries and Baptist colleges. These may involve short-term sessions of a single week or the one-month study programs now available in several seminaries. Midwestern seminary, for example, utilizes the one-month plan for all of its course work. Southern seminary offers three one-month terms in January, June, and July. Occasionally a director of missions may be able to arrange a four-month leave of absence for a full semester of study on campus. Short-term programs may be offered at Ridgecrest, Glorieta, the Church Program Training Center at the Sunday School Board, and special training sessions sponsored by the Home Mission Board and other denominational agencies. Other possibilities include programs available at universities and through their extension programs and in conferences conducted by management training personnel in business and industry.

C. *Areas needing attention.* Continuing education for directors of missions should give attention to a number of administrative and professional skills.

1. *Understanding and assisting pastors and church leaders.* The director of missions should be an expert in human resources development. He should understand the problems that pastors face and know well the individual ministers and their particular needs.

2. *Principles and procedures of counseling.* The director of missions must be a good listener. Growing out of his own self-understanding, he should be able to counsel others in discovering their potentialities, their strengths and weaknesses, and guide them in the solution of problems. Whenever he discovers problems greater than his own counseling skills, he should know where to refer for adequate help.

3. *Dealing with conflict and tension.* The director of missions will

often be called upon to resolve conflicts and deal with tension arising in the churches and in associational programs.

4. *Effective administrative procedures.* The director of missions needs to know principles and procedures in effective administration and be able to lead the ministers and other church leaders to discover needs; make careful plans; establish appropriate organizations; enlist and train leaders; administer effective programs through initiation, delegation, supervision, and motivation, coordinating, communicating, budgeting, providing adequate facilities, guiding comprehensive evaluation.

5. *Understanding organizations, how they work and how they may be utilized to achieve the programs of the association and the churches.*

6. *Understanding church educational programs and developing procedures for assisting the churches by making available the total resources of the various denominational agencies.*

7. *Discovering and relating the association and the churches to community needs.*

8. *Skills in office and property management, developing skills enabling the director of missions to counsel churches regarding buildings and furnishings.*

9. *Provision of supplementary studies in biblical, theological, and historical fields to help the director maintain his own abilities as minister and preacher.*

10. *Training to enable the director to give guidance to the continuing education of ministers and other church leaders in the association.*

D. *Responsibility and support.* The association should assume primary responsibility for providing financial support, time within the work schedule of the director of missions and encouragement toward participation to the point of including involvement in continuing education as a part of the director of missions' job description. Groups responsible for the selection of a director of missions should investigate the participation in continuing education programs by those being considered for the position. The associational budget provides for participation of the director of missions in continuing education. Salary increases might well be related in part to satisfactory fulfillment of annual continuing education programs.

Hopefully, Southern Baptists will develop within the next decade a strong interest in and adequate support for continuing education by the employing organization, whether it is a church, an association, or a denominational organization at the state or national level. Provision for continuing education should become one of the standard fringe benefits for ministers and denominational leaders.

Among the Southern Baptist Convention agencies in light of existing program assignments, the Home Mission Board would appear to have the major responsibility for providing counsel, financial assistance, and encouragement for continuing education opportunities for the director of missions. The HMB is particularly helpful in providing a Basic Leadership Seminar for New directors of mission that encourage the development of a continuing education plan with and for each director of missions utilizing various resources available in the course of his career.

The seminaries have a peculiar opportunity and responsibility to provide learning experiences including short-term courses, conferences, and degree programs. Such programs may be sponsored jointly with some other denominational agency, such as the HMB or the Sunday School Board. The Seminary Extension Department can offer valuable assistance through its home study courses, extension center courses, and the special continuing education series involving guided reading, cassette tapes, et cetera.

Other SBC agencies can be helpful. The Sunday School Board, WMU, and Brotherhood can assist in giving orientation to church programs, noting various resources available in their several departments and current plans for promoting church educational programs. The Foreign Mission Board and Home Mission Board may well offer assistance in the director of missions' work of developing mission awareness and encouraging greater financial support for missions.

Participation and promotion of continuing education by the director of missions may help set the pattern and lead the way to a new day in effective leadership among Southern Baptists.

10. The Director of Missions Satisfactions

The work of the director of missions is often complex and difficult. It can also be very rewarding and satisfying. Some will find their greatest satisfactions in their counseling and shepherding ministry. Some will rejoice when they have been able to encourage and inspire a despairing Christian leader to carry forward more effectively the work God has called him or her to do. Other directors of missions will find their greatest joy in their preaching ministry as they share in many different congregations the good news of the gospel. Some will rejoice most in their teaching ministry as they see those they have taught, whether in private conferences, small groups or in larger gatherings, undertake the work of the Kingdom with greater insight and skill. To see new missions established, new churches organized, mission giving increased, and churches strengthened will bring abiding satisfaction to many directors of missions. The ministry of administration brings enduring satisfactions to many as they see the total organization of the association on achieving the basic objectives for which it was brought into being.

One mark of effective leadership is the widespread distribution of satisfaction among the staff members of the association, the officers and organization leaders, and all the participants in the various activities and programs of the association. An association is likely to be working best when individual leaders are experiencing genuine satisfaction in their work and when the whole operation is bringing group satisfaction to the groups of people involved. One of the laws of learning is that people tend to repeat what they find satisfying and learn more as they repeat satisfying experiences.

The effective director of missions will be able to integrate the often divergent goals of individuals and groups in the association with the overall goals and objectives of the entire association.

To see individuals grow spiritually, to see lost people brought to Christ, to see churches develop in strength in their sense of purpose and direction, to see mission needs being met, lives being changed, the hungry being fed, the neglected and exploited in the community being cared for and helped, and the gospel being proclaimed effectively at home and abroad, these and other results from associational programs bring enduring satisfactions to the director of missions and all who work with him.

Although every director of missions should be regularly engaged in personal Christian ministries of witnessing, counseling and ministering, as an administrator the director of missions works largely with and through other people. Most of his satisfactions will be derived from what other people about him can be helped to do, from seeing the way others grow and develop in their Christian life, from helping individuals and groups to achieve satisfaction in the work they are doing, whether it be Bible teaching, witnessing, ministering to needy groups in the community, helping churches to be all that God expects, and sharing in the worldwide work of the kingdom of God.

The director of missions rightly rejoices in the accomplishments of the association but it is better to give others the credit for those achievements. If he has wrought well, many individuals, many churches, and many groups will have shared in the accomplishments. Appreciation should be expressed generously to these who have helped make any worthwhile achievements possible. Gratitude to God for the opportunity of service and the strength and wisdom required to accomplish the work God gives to do will ever be characteristic of the faithful servant of God who is serving as a director of missions out of the conviction that this is God's divine call for him.

NOTES

1. E. C. Watson, *Superintendent of Missions for an Association* (Atlanta: Home Mission Board, 1969), pp. 43–45.

2. J. C. Bradley, "A Transactional Theory of Church Administration" (Ed.D.

diss., Southern Baptist Theological Seminary, Louisville, Kentucky, 1969), p. 170f.

3. The director should find very helpful the suggestions in Brooks R. Faulkner, *Getting on Top of Your Work* (Nashville: Convention Press, 1973).

4. *Annual Associational Planning Guide,* Division of Associational Services, HMB (Atlanta: Home Mission Board, 1977), p. 3. See also Section IV, "Resources," for currently available printed resource materials and services from various Baptist agencies.

5. Lyle E. Schaller, *The Change Agent* (Nashville: Abingdon Press, 1972), p. 174.

6. *Ibid.*, pp. 175–176.

7. Elaine Dickson, "An Analysis of the Change Agent Function in Church Organization" (Ed.D. diss., Southern Baptist Theological Seminary, Louisville, Kentucky, 1972), p. 172.

8. *Ibid.*, p. 176.

9. *Ibid.*, p. 177.

Bibliography

Adams, Arthur M. *Pastoral Administration*. Philadelphia: Westminster Press, 1964.

Annual Associational Planning Guide. Division of Associational Services, HMB. Atlanta: Home Mission Board, 1974.

Associational Strategy Planning Guide. Division of Associational Services, HMB. Atlanta: Home Mission Board, 1974.

Bennis, Warren G.; Benne, Kenneth D.; and Chin, Robert. *The Planning of Change*. New York: Hold, Rinehart and Winston, 1969.

Bennis, Warren G.; and Slater, Philip E. *The Temporary Society*. New York: Harper-Row, 1968.

Bradley, J. C. "A Transactional Theory of Church Administration." (Ed.D. diss., Southern Baptist Theological Seminary, Louisville, Kentucky, 1969):

Buchanan, Edward A. *Developing Leadership Skills*. Nashville: Convention Press, 1971.

Cromer, William R. *Introduction to Church Leadership*. Nashville: Convention Press, 1971.

Cumbie, William J. "Baptist Polity: A Survey of Issues and Trends from the Associational Perspective," *Search*. I, 2, Winter, 1971.

Cyert, R. M.; and March, J. G. *A Behavioral Theory of the Firm*. New Jersey: Prentice-Hall, 1963.

Daniel, James; and Dickson, Elaine, eds. *The 70's, Opportunities for Your Churches*. Nashville: Convention Press, 1969.

Dickson, Elaine. "An Analysis of the Change Agent Function in Church Organization." (Ed.D. diss., Southern Baptist Theological Seminary, Louisville, Kentucky, 1972).

Principles of Administration

Dobbins, Gaines S. *Learning to Lead*. Nashville: Broadman Press, 1968.

Dowis, S. F. *Associational Guidebook*. Nashville: Convention Press, 1959.

Etzioni, Amitai. *A Sociological Reader on Complex Organizations*. New York: Holt, Rinehart and Winston, 1969.

Etzioni, Amitai. *Modern Organizations*. Englewood Cliffs: Prentice-Hall, 1964.

Eddy, William B., ed. *Behaviora! Sciences and the Manager's Role*. Washington, D.C.: National Training Laboratories' Institute for Applied Behavioral Science, 1969.

Faulkner, Brooks R. *Getting on Top of Your Work*. Nashville: Convention Press, 1973.

Gerth, H. H., and Mills, C. Wright, eds. and trans. "Bureaucracy," English translation in *From Max Weber, Essays in Sociology*. New York: Oxford University Press, 1946.

Hersey, Paul, and Blanchard, Kenneth H. *The Management of Organizational Behavior: Utilizing Human Resources*. Englewood Cliffs: Prentice-Hall, 1972.

Johns, Ray. *Executive Responsibility*. New York: Association Press, 1966.

May, Lynn E., Jr. *The Work of the Baptist Association, An Integrative Study*. Atlanta: Home Mission Board, 1969.

McCall, Duke K. "Is Absolute Autonomy Desirable," *Search*. I, 2, Winter, 1971.

McClellan, Albert. "The Challenge of Associational Administration." (Unpublished address, February, 1970).

McGlothlin, W. J. *Baptist Confession of Faith*. Valley Forge: American Baptist Publications Society, 1911.

McGregor, Douglas. *The Human Side of Enterprise*. New York: McGraw-Hill, 1960.

Metz, Donald L. *New Congregations, Security and Mission in Conflict*. Philadelphia: Westminster Press, 1967.

Oates, Wayne E. *The Holy Spirit in Five Worlds*. New York: Association Press, 1968.

Perrow, Charles. *Organizational Analysis: A Sociological View*. Belmont: Brooks-Cole Publishing Company, 1970.

Report of Conference on Associational Missions, February 11-15, 1963. Gulfshore Baptist Assembly. Atlanta: Home Mission Board, 1963.

Rose, Morton F. Unpublished seminar paper. Southern Baptist Theological Seminary, Louisville, Kentucky, October 23, 1973.

Rudge, Peter F. *Ministry and Management*. New York: Barnes and Noble, 1970.

Bibliography

Schaller, Lyle E. "The Anticipatory Style," *The Christian Ministry*. III, 3, May, 1972.

Schaller, Lyle E. *The Change Agent*. Nashville: Abingdon Press, 1972.

Schlesinger, Arthur M., Jr. *A Thousand Days*. Boston: Houghton-Mifflin, 1965.

Von Bertalannfy, Ludwig. *General System Theory: Foundations, Development, Applications*. New York: George Braziller, Inc., 1969.

Watson, E. C. *Associational Base Design*. Atlanta: Home Mission Board, 1972.

Watson, E. C. *Superintendent of Missions for an Association*. Atlanta: Home Mission Board, 1969.